THEY OWN THE NIGHT
SURVIVING THE PILLIGA

LUKA T. JACOBS
&
MICHELLE FORD

Cover Design, Book Design & Formatting:
Luka T. Jacobs.

Copyright © 2024 Luka T. Jacobs. All rights reserved. No portion of this book may be reproduced in any form without written permission from the publisher or author, except as permitted by U.S. copyright law.

All photography in this book use the Creative Commons licence https://creativecommons.org/licenses/by/2.0/.

ISBN: 978-1-7637809-8-9

DEDICATION

....

Thank you, as always, to my partner Adam and my little guy Finnigan. I also want to acknowledge Michelle Ford for her strength and resilience in writing her book, which I had the privilege of helping with.

LUKA T. JACOBS

Thank you to my family and my husband for your continued support and patience (and for not thinking I was crazy).

MICHELLE FORD

TABLE OF CONTENTS

PREFACE		9
PROLOGUE WHY I WROTE THIS BOOK		13
1	THE BEGINNING	17
2	CREEPING SENSE OF FEAR	21
3	HAND PRINT	25
4	LOTS OF WILDLIFE HERE	29
5	LIKE ROTTING MEAT	33
6	PILLIGA HISTORY	37
7	COULD BE A TRAP	41
8	MONKEY FACE	45
9	MORE THAN ONE	49
10	NEIGHBOUR'S ENCOUNTERS	53
11	THE OPEN DOOR	57
12	PANIC ATTACK	61
13	HOWLS	65
14	GETTING BOLDER	69
15	ROCK THROWING	73
16	DAMNED IF YOU DO	75
17	THE OFFERING	77

18	THAT DIDN'T GO TO PLAN	79
19	CUNNING BASTARDS	83
20	BLOOD RUNS COLD	87
21	STAY QUIET	91
22	SCREAMING IN TERROR	95
23	A FEW DAYS REPRIEVE	99
24	IT SNARLED	103
25	SAFETY ABOVE ALL	105
26	MONSTER	107
27	WE CAN'T WAIT ANY LONGER	111
EPILOGUE 1	MOVING ON	113
EPILOGUE 2	WHY WE DIDN'T RECORD EVIDENCE	115
AUTHOR BIO		117
EMBRACE THE MYSTERY WEAR THE LEGEND		119
SNEAK PEAK – NIGHT OF THE DOGMAN: THE SCENT		121
SNEAK PEAK – NIGHT OF THE DOGMAN: A STRANGE SIGHTING		125

Yowie in the Australian bush. Illustration by Luka T. Jacobs.

PREFACE

......

In June of 2022, we, the Ford family, packed up our lives and moved to a small homestead on the outskirts of the Pilliga in New South Wales, Australia. It was a leap of faith, driven by necessity and a yearning for a simpler, more sustainable life. Ballina, with its constant hum of tourists, had been our home for years. However, no matter how hard Ted and I worked, we could never seem to get ahead. Ted, a truck driver, spent countless hours on the road, while I balanced part-time data entry work from home with raising our two children, Rachel and James, who were then 5 and 7, respectively.

Life in Ballina had its comforts, but it was expensive. We had grown tired of the relentless grind, the feeling of treading water but never reaching shore. Ted grew up in Moree and I hailed from Cootamundra, small towns that had instilled in us an appreciation for the countryside and its slower pace. We longed for a place where the air was clear, the land was open, and we could afford to breathe without the constant worry of making ends meet.

The decision to move wasn't easy, but it was necessary. We scoured listings, looking for a place that offered us a fresh start without breaking the bank. When we found the farmstead, it seemed perfect. Nestled on the edge of the sprawling Pilliga Forest, it promised space for the kids to run, a garden to grow our food, and a tranquility we had only dreamed of in Ballina. We decided to rent the house initially, not wanting to commit to buying a property in a completely new area without seeing if we could fit in first.

The day we arrived, the sun was setting, casting a golden glow over the landscape. Our new home was modest but charming, with a weathered barn and a porch that creaked underfoot. Rachel and James were thrilled, exploring every nook and cranny, their laughter echoing through the fields. Ted and I stood hand in hand, feeling a rare sense of peace. This was our fresh start, our chance to build something better for our family.

But it wasn't long before we realised we weren't alone. It started with small things—shadows in the night, the feeling of being watched, strange noises. At first, we brushed it off as the stress of moving and our imaginations running wild in the unfamiliar surroundings.

However, soon, it became impossible to ignore.

Our journey had brought us here for a reason. Whether it was to confront our fears, to find peace, or to build a life worth living, we were determined to make it work. Little did we know, our adventure was just beginning, and the secrets of the Pilliga were waiting to reveal themselves.

SURVIVING THE PILLIGA

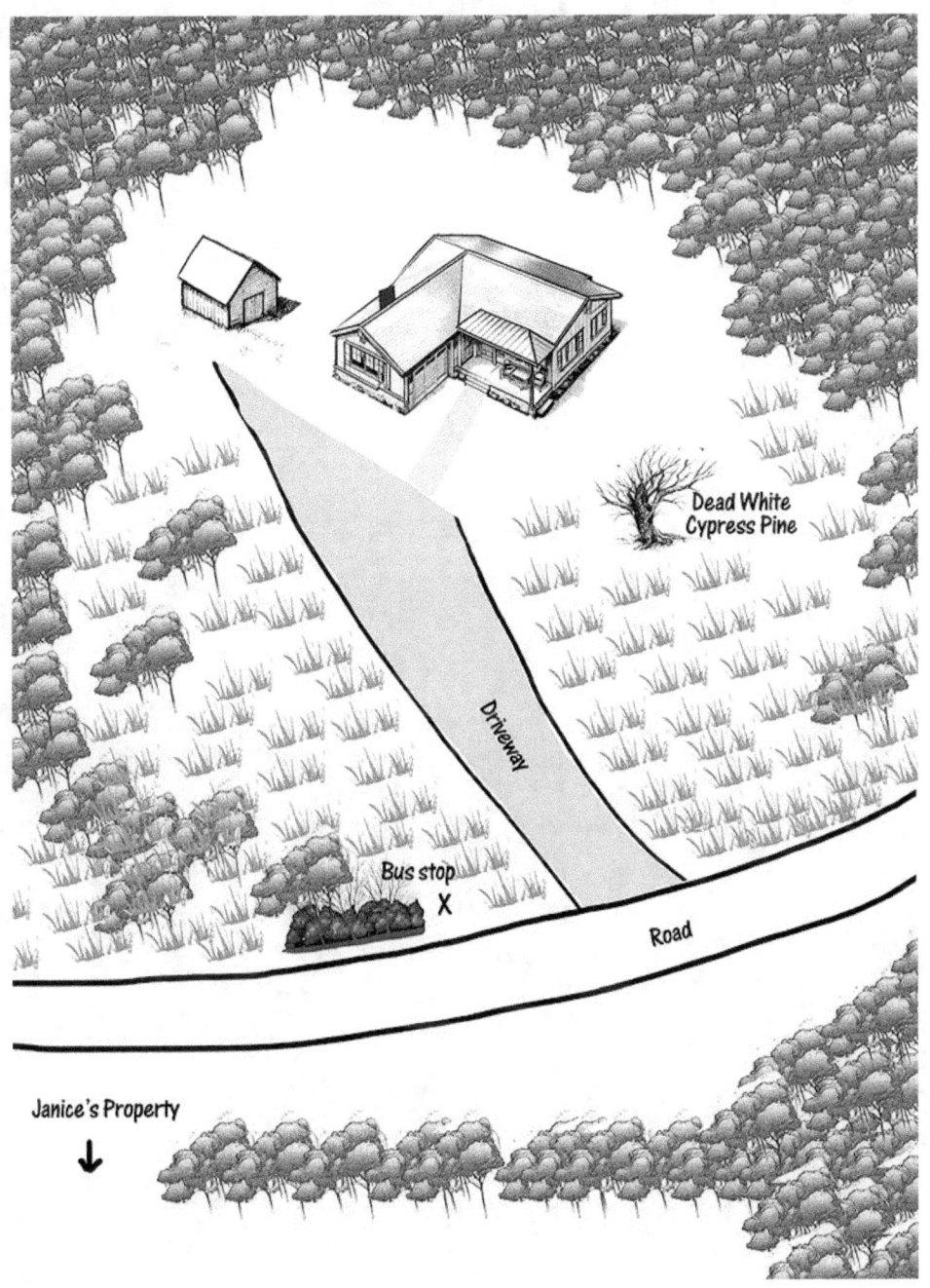

My crude drawing of our homestead.

PROLOGUE

WHY I WROTE THIS BOOK

It's a question I've asked myself countless times as I sit here, staring at the blinking cursor on my laptop screen. For a long time, I wanted nothing more than to forget what happened at the homestead in the Pilliga, to bury those memories deep and never speak of them again. I have to admit, though, when things first started happening, I did question my sanity. Many times.

Only our immediate family knows the full story. My husband Ted, along with Rachel and James, lived through it with me, and they bear the same scars. When we shared our experience with our family, most of them believed us, though some were hesitant to accept such a tale. "Maybe the stress of the pandemic and the move has taken a toll on your mental health," one family member suggested.

My parents were an absolute godsend and supported us without hesitation.

For months, I struggled to move on. I experienced frequent panic attacks and often woke up in the middle of the night, gasping for air with my heart racing. I told myself it was over, that we were safe, and that it was best to let sleeping dogs lie (or sleeping Yowies, rather). But the memories lingered, haunting the edges of my mind like shadows refusing to dissipate with the dawn.

It was my sister who suggested that I write everything down, saying it would be therapeutic—a way to exorcise the ghosts of our past and find some semblance of peace. She even suggested that I share my experiences on a podcast, but the thought of talking about them in real-time made me feel nauseous. I doubted I could do that. As she became fascinated with the subject, she joined several Facebook groups about the Yowie and Bigfoot. Through one of those groups, she met Luka, the co-author of this book.

At first, I resisted. How could reliving those terrifying days and nights possibly help? But one day, the weight of it all became too much to bear. I emailed Luka, and from there, she was an unbelievable help in turning my family's experiences into a book. Thank you, Luka, for all your help and guidance—I couldn't have done it without you.

To my surprise, putting the events into words did help. It allowed me to process the trauma and make sense of the chaos that had turned our lives upside down. I have fewer panic attacks now, and when I do, I can calm myself much quicker (it also helps to now live in the suburbs with thousands of homes between us and the bush).

I had no idea that these creatures existed. Of course, in my 36 years, I had heard about Yowies—particularly the American version, Bigfoot—but it never entered my mind that I would ever come across something like this in my life.

Some people say that Yowies are peaceful beings, more curious than anything else. That may be true for some. I can only assume they have different personalities, like humans, shaped by their unique experiences. Unfortunately, the Yowies on our property were anything but peaceful.

Now, as I write this, I feel ready to share our story. To finally put those days and nights of terror behind us and move on to better things. I find it a strange sense of release, as if unburdening myself of a weight I've carried for too long.

I know it might sound unbelievable. It doesn't bother me if you don't believe me, and I am certainly not here to convince anyone that these monsters exist. All I am here to do is share my story, to put the truth out there in the hope that someone else who has experienced similar things might find comfort in knowing they aren't alone.

If you're looking for a book filled with monsters, blood, and gore, this is not it. However, if you seek an honest account of our experience living with Yowies, then please, read on.

This experience has changed me forever, and I look at the world in a completely different way now.

Michelle xx

P.S. Luka and I went through numerous revisions of the Yowie drawing on the cover, striving to capture it as accurately as possible to match what Ted and I saw. She did such a wonderful job that it is hard for me to look at.

1

THE BEGINNING

A few days after we moved in, the kids' rooms were mostly unpacked, their toys and clothes finding new homes in our old homestead. Ted and I, on the other hand, still had boxes stacked in the corners of our bedroom and the living room, filled with everything that wasn't an immediate necessity.

It was a quiet Tuesday night. After a simple but satisfying dinner with the family, I stood at the kitchen sink, washing dishes. The rhythmic sound of water running, and the clinking of plates provided a comforting background noise. The kids' laughter echoed faintly from the living room, mingling with the soft hum of the night outside.

As I gazed out the window, an eerie stillness settled over the farm. Little did I know, this tranquil evening was about to mark the beginning of an extraordinary and terrifying chapter in our lives.

The window above the sink overlooked the yard and the barn beyond. The moon was bright that night, casting a silvery glow over the landscape. I was lost in thought, my hands moving automatically as I scrubbed plates and utensils. It was a rare moment of peace in our otherwise chaotic life.

As I rinsed a plate, I caught movement out of the corner of my eye. I looked up quickly and saw a humanoid figure on the roof of the barn. It was dark, tall, and slim, moving with an unsettling grace. Before I could fully process what I was seeing, the figure ran to the back of the barn and seemingly jumped off. It happened so quickly that I wasn't sure if I had imagined it.

My first instinct was to assume it was a person on our barn roof. I opened my mouth to call out for Ted, but then I hesitated. The figure had been extremely tall, much taller than any person I knew, and it had moved with an unnatural speed. It hadn't just run—it had glided across the roof and then jumped off a height of at least 10-12 feet without hesitation. The sight was so bizarre and terrifying that my mind struggled to make sense of it.

I stood there, frozen, staring out into the dark yard. My heart pounded in my chest, and my hands were still in the soapy water. I didn't know if I should tell Ted. The thought of him going out there in the dark, with no lights on that side of the house yet, filled me with dread. I remained at the sink, unable to move, my eyes fixed on the barn, searching for any sign of the figure.

The sound of the kids arguing in the living room finally broke my trance. I stepped away from the sink and sat down at the dining table, trying to collect my thoughts. Ted was glued to the TV, oblivious to my distress (and the kids arguing, apparently). I replayed the sighting in my mind over and over, trying to rationalise it. Maybe it was a trick of the light or a shadow cast by the moon. But deep down, I knew I had seen something.

Eventually, I went back to the sink to finish the dishes, my movements slow and deliberate. I closed the blinds, not wanting to see whatever was out there. After finishing, I sat down on the couch next to Ted and mentioned that I thought I saw something on the roof of the barn. He glanced at me, half-interested, and asked if it was a possum or something. I shook my head, trying to find the words to explain.

"It was more like a human," I said, "but extremely tall and dressed in dark clothing. It moved so fast."

Ted laughed softly, dismissing my concerns. "You must have been daydreaming or seeing things," he said, his attention already back on the TV.

Frustrated and unsettled, I got up and went into the bathroom to wash my face. The cold water did little to calm my nerves. I went to bed early, but sleep was elusive. I lay there, tossing and turning, my mind racing with thoughts of what I had seen. Every creak and groan of the old house set my nerves on edge.

The night stretched on, each minute feeling like an hour. I kept replaying the sighting in my mind, trying to understand it. What had I seen? And more importantly, what did it want? Had it been sitting there watching me? A shiver ran down my spine at the thought. If it was just a human, why did seeing it disturb me so deeply?

I finally drifted off to a restless sleep just before dawn, haunted by dreams of dark, gliding figures and the unsettling sense that our new home held more secrets than we had ever imagined.

The next morning, I woke up feeling drained. Ted had already left for a truck run, and the kids were getting ready for school. The memory of the previous night's sighting weighed heavily on me, but I decided to keep it to myself for now. Ted's reaction had made it clear he wouldn't take me seriously, and I didn't want to scare the kids.

As I went about my day, the unease lingered but I tried to put it to the back of mind, telling myself that it was a trick of the light and I had just been overwhelmed with the move. What the heck else could it be?

2

CREEPING SENSE OF FEAR

A few days later, after noting that not much had happened, I was awoken at around 2 a.m. by what I thought were bird calls. They sounded like galahs, but there was something off—more mechanical, almost like a recording. As I lay there, trying to shake off the sleep, I realised that someone, or something, was mimicking the bird sounds. But why? It was the middle of the night, and even though I had grown up on a semi-rural property, I had never heard galahs at this hour before.

One call came from behind our house and was answered by another near the barn.

I lay in bed, listening intently for about twenty minutes. Curiosity mingled with a creeping sense of fear. If these sounds were being made by people, they were on our property without permission. The thought that they might know Ted wasn't home and that I was alone with the kids unsettled me. I tried to reassure myself that the house was locked up tight and eventually drifted back to sleep.

The next morning, as I was about to put a load of washing out on the line, I stepped out the back door and headed down the steps. That's when I noticed the footprints in the soil next to the stairs. These were no ordinary footprints. They were massive.

My heart raced as I followed the trail. The footprints circled around the left side of the house and led to the steps at the front of the porch. I stood there, hands on my hips, staring at them, when a strange sensation tickled the back of my neck and shot down my spine. I looked up, my head swiveling, but I couldn't see anyone. Still, I felt eyes on me.

Feeling vulnerable even in broad daylight, I hurriedly hung out the laundry, constantly glancing over my shoulder. I had never seen footprints that big before, and they were bare feet. If there had been teenagers making those bird calls last night, wouldn't they be wearing shoes? No way would I be out at night without shoes, especially in a place where you could easily step on a snake or a sharp rock. But then again, kids were known for acting without thinking.

Besides, we lived out in the boondocks, with our nearest neighbour at least 2 klms away. It wasn't like there were kids up and down the block.

Suddenly I remembered the figure on the barn roof, the bird noises from the night before, and now these footprints. A rising sense of unease washed over me. What the heck was going on here? Did someone want us out of this place, or was I just going crazy?

As I walked back into the house, my mind raced with possibilities. I decided it was time to talk to Ted about everything that had been happening, even if he might brush it off again. The kids were already up, eating breakfast, oblivious to the strange events unfolding around them.

I called Ted, needing to share my growing unease. "Hey, can you talk?" I asked as soon as he answered.

"Sure, what's up?" he replied.

I took a deep breath and recounted everything—the figure on the barn roof, the mechanical bird calls, and the massive footprints. There was a long pause on the other end of the line.

"Look, it's probably just some local kids playing a prank," Ted finally said. "You know how they can be, especially if they hear there's a new family in the area."

"But Ted," I insisted, "the footprints were huge and barefoot. And the noises at night... it didn't sound like kids. And who would walk around here without shoes?"

"I don't know," he said, sounding more thoughtful. "Maybe it's just some kind of local wildlife we're not familiar with. Or an animal with unusual behavior. There could be a logical explanation."

"But what about the figure on the barn roof?" I pressed. "That wasn't an animal."

"You're right," he admitted. "I don't have a good explanation for that. If it happens again, call the police. I will be home in a few days," he finally said. "In the meantime, keep the doors and windows locked. Don't go outside at night."

"Okay," I agreed, feeling a bit more reassured but still uneasy. "Just hurry home, please."

"I will," Ted promised. "You will be ok."

As I hung up the phone, the sense of unease lingered, but knowing Ted would be home soon gave me some comfort. I wasn't 100% sure that he believed me, maybe he just heard the tone in my voice and knew I was genuinely scared. I wasn't normally an emotional person.

I tried to go about my day, but the unease lingered. I couldn't shake the feeling that something was watching us, something that didn't belong in our world. The kids were already up, eating breakfast, oblivious to the strange events unfolding around them.

That night, I stayed up late, making sure all the doors and windows were securely locked. I eventually fell asleep in the early hours and had my first decent sleep in days.

3

HAND PRINT

The next few days passed uneventfully, but the sense of being watched never left me. I was constantly on edge, jumping at every little sound. Ted tried to reassure me over the phone, but I could tell he was just as unsettled.

Finally, Ted returned home. The relief I felt seeing him walk through the door was overwhelming. I threw my arms around him, holding on tightly, as if afraid he might disappear. He hugged me back, sensing my fear.

"You need to feel safe in your own home," he said firmly. "I'll set up security cameras around the property tomorrow."

That night, as we sat in the living room discussing our plan, a loud thud echoed from outside. My heart leaped into my throat. Ted grabbed a flashlight and stood up, ready to investigate.

"Please, be careful," I whispered, my voice barely audible over the pounding of my heart.

He nodded and headed out the door. I watched from the window, my hands pressed against the glass, eyes straining to see through the darkness. The beam of his flashlight cut through the night, illuminating the path to the barn. Every second felt like an eternity as I waited, my mind racing with worst-case scenarios.

Ted moved cautiously, the flashlight beam dancing across the ground. He scanned the area around the barn but then paused by the car. I saw him lean in, peering closely at something on the driver's side window. He straightened up, his face pale in the moonlight, and hurried back to the house.

"What did you find?" I asked, my voice shaking.

Ted locked the door behind him and took a deep breath. "There's a huge hand print on the driver's side window," he said quietly. "It's too dark to get a good look at it now. I'll check it out properly in the morning."

We stood there for a moment, the gravity of his words sinking in. Something—or someone—was out there, watching us, and it wasn't going away.

The next morning, Ted and I went outside to check the hand print on the window. As it was winter, there was still some frost on the windows, but you could clearly see the hand print in the daylight. It was enormous—at least 2.5 times the size of Ted's hand, and Ted stood at 6'2". The print had a greasy feel to it, unlike anything we had ever encountered.

Ted spent the afternoon setting up cameras around the property, focusing on the areas where we had seen the footprints and heard the noises. As he worked, I couldn't shake the feeling that we were being watched, that unseen eyes were on us, observing our every move. Maybe I was just being paranoid?

I sat on the porch, helping Ted whenever he needed it, while making sure the kids stayed inside. It bothered me to keep them indoors since we had moved here to give them more time outside in the fresh air, yet here we were, telling them not to come outside. They were curious but content to get more free time on their devices.

"Ted, do you think the cameras will catch anything?" I asked, trying to keep my voice steady.

He looked up from adjusting a camera. "I hope so," he said, wiping sweat from his brow. "At the very least, it might give us some answers—or at least some peace of mind."

We continued setting up the cameras, each movement deliberate and careful. The sun began to set, casting long shadows across the yard. The sense of being watched never left me, and I could tell Ted felt it too.

That night, as we reviewed the setup and made sure everything was working, we both felt a glimmer of hope. Maybe, just maybe, we would finally understand what was haunting our new home and take steps to protect our family.

We went to bed feeling a bit more secure, knowing we would at least have some way of seeing what was out there. But deep down, I couldn't shake the feeling that we were dealing with something beyond the ordinary. I opened the security camera app on my phone and watched the footage while Ted snored beside me. He was due to go back out on a run in a weeks time, and I hoped whatever or whoever was outside would move on by then.

As I lay there in bed, I couldn't help but wonder if someone—or something—wanted us gone. The thought lingered in the back of my mind, refusing to be dismissed.

We had come here seeking peace and a fresh start, but it seemed that the farmstead had other plans for us. And as much as I wanted to believe otherwise, the unsettling feeling that we were not alone remained.

4

LOTS OF WILDLIFE HERE

The next morning, I skimmed through the recordings from the previous night while the kids ate breakfast. Ted had left to get his car looked at by the mechanic. As I watched the footage, a sense of unease settled over me. There were strange noises and fleeting shadows, but nothing concrete. Determined to get to the bottom of the mystery, I decided to talk to the neighbours and see if they knew what could be going on around our property.

Our property spanned 20 acres, and the neighbouring properties were even larger. We had two neighbours on either side and one across the road a little way down. I decided to start with the neighbour across the road, an older lady named Janice. We had heard she had a reputation for being a bit gruff, but I hoped she might have some insight.

I walked the kids down our long driveway and waited with them for the bus. Once they were safely on their way, I headed over to Janice's place. Unlike in the suburbs we were used to, the walk took a good ten minutes.

When I knocked on her door, Janice opened it with a half-scowl, half-smile—a curious expression I wasn't sure how to interpret. "Hello, I'm Michelle, your neighbour from across the road," I said, extending my hand.

Janice looked at my hand for a moment before shaking it. "Nice to meet you, Michelle. Would you like a coffee? We can sit on the patio."

I agreed, and she led me to the patio lounge while she went to get the coffees. As I waited, I looked around her property. It was well-kept, with a beautiful garden and a stunning view of the surrounding countryside. It was hard to imagine anything sinister happening here. She had far fewer trees and shrubs surrounding her home than we did.

Janice returned with two mugs of coffee and handed me one. "So, what brings you over this morning?" she asked, settling into her chair.

I took a sip of the coffee, savouring the warmth before answering. "Well, we've noticed some strange things happening around our property. Odd noises, large footprints, that sort of thing. I was wondering if you or anyone else in the area has experienced anything similar?"

Janice's expression didn't change, but I noticed a flicker of something—was it recognition?—in her eyes. She took a long sip of her coffee before replying. "Oh, you know how it is in the countryside. Lots of wildlife out here. Could be anything."

Her nonchalant response didn't convince me. "I understand that, but these footprints were huge. And the noises... they don't sound like any animal I've ever heard."

Janice shifted in her seat, avoiding my gaze. "Well, it's an old area with a lot of history. There are bound to be some unexplained things. Best not to dwell on it too much."

I pressed on, hoping to get more out of her. "Janice, have you ever heard of Yowies?"

She stiffened slightly, her eyes narrowing. "Yowies? Just old wives' tales, if you ask me. People love to tell stories, especially around here. Makes life a bit more interesting."

I could tell she was trying to deflect. "But you've heard the stories?"

Janice sighed, setting her glass down on the table. "Look, Michelle, I don't want to scare you. You're new here, and it's easy to let your imagination run wild. Just keep an eye on things and stay safe. That's all anyone can do."

It was clear she didn't want to discuss it further, so I let the subject drop. We chatted a bit more about the local area, and she gave me some tips on where to find the best produce and which trails were good for hiking. Despite her initial gruffness, she was pleasant enough once we got talking.

As I left, I couldn't shake the feeling that Janice knew more than she was letting on. Her reluctance to talk about the strange occurrences on our property only fuelled my curiosity. What was she hiding? And why didn't she want me to know about the Yowies?

I decided to visit the other neighbours in the coming days to see if they had any insights. For now, I had more questions than answers. But one thing was certain—I wasn't going hiking on any bush trails, no matter how good they were!

So many places for a Yowie to hide. <u>Photo by Hugh Nicholson</u>.

5

LIKE ROTTING MEAT

Back at home, after finishing some chores, I reviewed the recordings again while sitting on the porch, searching for any clue I might have missed. The kids were back from school, playing in the yard in front of me, their laughter a stark contrast to the eerie events that had unfolded. I knew I had to protect them, but first, I needed to understand what we were dealing with.

Ted returned from the mechanic later that day, and I told him about my visit with Janice. He frowned, clearly concerned. "We'll figure this out, Michelle," he said, squeezing my hand. "Whatever it takes."

His reassurance bolstered my resolve just a little. I decided to do a few hours of work before starting dinner.

That night, we were all sitting on the couch watching TV when a foul smell suddenly hit my nose. I assumed it was Ted and threw a cushion at him playfully. He looked at me, shocked.

"What?" he asked.

"Thanks for stinking up the place," I replied, teasingly.

"It wasn't me," Ted insisted. As I turned to ask the kids if they were responsible, Ted started smelling it too, followed by the kids. The odour was so pungent and heavy, it felt like it would never go away. It was a thick, nauseating smell, reminiscent of old garbage or rotting meat. The kids laughed and coughed at the stench.

I thought surely such a smell couldn't have come from one of us. Then I noticed the large window to the right of the TV was slightly open, with the blinds barely covering it. I looked at Ted, who was burying his head in the pillow I had thrown at him and motioned towards the window with my head. He gave me a puzzled look, then glanced at the open window.

"Maybe it's coming from outside," I whispered, careful not to let the kids hear.

Ted mouthed to me to just ignore it, and that's what we tried to do. I knew the doors were locked, and I felt much safer with Ted there. I tried to focus on the TV, but the unsettling feeling lingered. Eventually, I got up to close the window and retreated to the study to continue working, though I found it hard to concentrate with the constant sense that something was off.

That night, we got the kids to bed with no hassle. I made sure their windows were closed and locked tight. The last thing I wanted was for something to get into their rooms. Ted checked the front and back doors before coming to bed. We discussed the awful smell from earlier, wondering what it could have been.

As Ted settled in, I checked the camera live feeds again and sat in bed staring at it. Part of me didn't want to see anything, yet another part of me did. I needed to know what we were dealing with.

Hours passed, and the house was silent except for the occasional creak of the old wood. I found myself drifting in and out of sleep, the camera app still open on my phone. Just as I was about to give up and put my phone down, a movement caught my eye. It was subtle, a shadow passing by one of the cameras near the barn.

I nudged Ted awake. "Look," I whispered, showing him the live camera feed.

He squinted at the phone, then his eyes widened. "What is that?" he asked.

"I don't know, but it's near the barn."

We watched for a few more minutes, but the shadow didn't reappear. Ted sighed and rubbed his eyes. "I'll check it out in the morning. Let's try to get some sleep."

Reluctantly, I agreed. We lay back down, but my mind kept replaying the events of the day—the strange smell, Janice's cryptic warnings, and now this shadow. Sleep came fitfully, filled with restless dreams of unseen watchers and lurking dangers.

The Pilliga is 35,632 hectares of wilderness. Photo by Dave Milledge.

6

PILLIGA HISTORY

Morning brought a sense of cautious normalcy. Ted and I exchanged uneasy glances as we went about our routine. After watching the kids walk down to the bus stop from the patio, Ted headed out to check the barn. I watched him through the kitchen window, my heart pounding as he disappeared into the shadows of the barn.

He emerged a few minutes later, shaking his head. "Nothing there," he called out. "No signs of anything unusual."

Relief mixed with frustration. I wanted answers, but they remained elusive. Determined to find out more, I turned to the internet to look up weird happenings in the Pilliga. To my surprise, countless stories and encounters mentioning the Yowie popped up.

Many accounts came from people who had camped overnight in the area. They described hearing eerie noises and encountering strange, shadowy figures that left massive footprints behind. Some even reported seeing "glowing red eyes" peering at them through the darkness.

One story that stood out was from a trucker who refused to drive through the Pilliga at night. He claimed to have seen a large, hairy creature crossing the road in front of his truck, emitting a foul smell and strange, guttural noises.

Another account from a family who had camped in the Pilliga described their encounter with a shadowy figure. They had also heard strange noises in the night and felt an overwhelming sense of being watched.

The more I read, the more convinced I became that something was indeed out there. These stories were often dismissed as folklore or the overactive imaginations of residents, but the patterns were undeniable. People from all walks of life had experienced similar strange occurrences, and many were deeply shaken by their encounters.

The similarities to what we had experienced were too striking to ignore as much as I didn't want to believe that Yowies were real, the truth was kind of smacking me in the face.

Armed with new information, I decided to visit our next-door neighbors to gather more details about our immediate area. The Raymonds lived about 2 kilometers north of us. As I drove towards their property, I noticed the property across from them looked like it was undergoing some work. Trucks were in the driveway, and there were a few tractors and a soil mound. I passed them and pulled into the Raymonds' property.

The Raymonds had a simple fibro home with old cars and parts littering the fields around their house. It was clear someone loved collecting cars but wasn't as keen on restoring them.

As I pulled up, Peter Raymond walked out onto the porch. He was a tall man in his late fifties, with greying hair and a rugged, weathered face that suggested years of hard work outdoors. His blue eyes, though sharp and attentive, held a hint of kindness. He wore a worn flannel shirt and faded jeans, adding to his rustic appearance. He watched as I got out of the car, and I introduced myself. With a firm handshake, he welcomed me into his home.

Peter already knew who I was (small towns, right?) and asked how we were liking the place. I confessed that we had experienced some strange happenings and mentioned a few of the incidents. Peter looked like he was about to say something but then stopped himself, choosing his words carefully.

"Have you met the Sipples who live across from me?" he asked, taking a deep breath.

"No," I replied, "but I noticed they were having some construction done as I drove by."

"Yes," he said, "they're building a new barn, but they've been having trouble there too. It started with small things like tools going missing or being moved around the yard. Then one morning, Merv Sipple came out to find one of the tractors used for moving dirt had been tipped over onto his water tank overnight. He was shocked that he didn't hear it. The next day, two of his workers quit, and the other two wanted to quit but couldn't afford to, so they agreed not to work past dusk."

I asked Peter if they knew what was causing all of this. He said Merv Sipple hadn't seen anything but suspected it was Yowies. I almost gasped. I couldn't believe someone else had mentioned them as the culprits. Heck, I still wasn't 100% convinced they even existed.

"Do you believe in them?" I asked Peter.

He nodded. "Yes. My mother's side of the family is First Nations, and they believe in the Yowie. Many clans live within the Pilliga."

Hearing this from Peter added a new layer to the mystery. It wasn't just folklore or the ramblings of an old neighbor. It was a belief deeply rooted in the culture of the area.

"Have you ever seen one?" I asked, my curiosity piqued.

He nodded. "Oh yes, when I was a child. I saw the same one a few times outside the bedroom window on my great-grandfather's property. It never caused any problems. It just stank a lot. A smell you never forget.

"My mother used to say the Yowies are guardians of the land. They are ancient beings, deeply connected to nature and the spiritual world. They protect the sacred sites and ensure that the land remains in balance."

He paused, looking out over the vast expanse of his property. "The elders say the Yowies have been here long before any of us. They have a deep respect for the earth and all its creatures. Disturbing their territory or harming the environment can provoke them. My grandmother used to tell us that the Yowies have their own paths and places they frequent. If those are disrupted, it can lead to the kind of incidents we've been seeing."

I pondered his words. If the Yowies were real and they were feeling threatened, what could be causing it? And why were they so active around our property and the Sipples'? Could the building of a new barn threaten them somehow?

I then asked Peter if he knew the previous tenants of our place. He replied, "Not really, they weren't there very long. They had a small family, similar to yours, and after about two weeks of living there, they upped and left one night without a word."

His words sent a chill down my spine. What had driven them away so suddenly? Was it the same thing we were now experiencing?

7

COULD BE A TRAP

As I drove back home, my mind raced with possibilities. The pieces of the puzzle were starting to come together, but there were still so many unanswered questions. I wasn't entirely convinced there were Yowies on our property, but everything did seem to be pointing to them.

After a few hours of work, I met the kids at the end of the driveway when they got off the bus. We walked up the driveway discussing what they had done at school. Rachel held my hand tight and was practically on top of me. I asked her if there was anything wrong and she said no. I didn't want to press it and knew she would tell me when she was ready.

The kids did their homework while I did a few more hours of work. It was getting harder to concentrate, even though I tried not to think of what could be outside our home.

I made dinner and we all sat down at the table to enjoy it and discuss the day. We had only been sitting down for a few minutes when we heard a loud bang at the back of the house.

I looked at Ted, who gave me a worried glance and got up from the table. I wanted to tell him to be careful, but I didn't want to alarm the kids. I just told them to keep eating and that it was probably a kangaroo that had hit the house. I hoped it was as simple as that.

Ted grabbed his flashlight, but before he went to the back door, I grabbed his arm and told him to wait a minute while I reviewed the camera footage. Pulling up the app, I selected the camera facing the backyard and replayed the last saved clip. Ted watched with me as we saw something fly across the screen and hit the back door. It seemed small, whatever it was. My stomach lurched at the sight.

"Don't go out there. Maybe it's a trap, hon. Let's wait until morning to see what it is," I suggested to Ted.

He looked at the back door and then me in the eyes and said, "Alright." I knew he wasn't happy with not knowing what was going on.

"I went and talked to the Raymonds next door today. We'll discuss it after the kids have gone to bed," I said.

Ted agreed, and we went back to eating dinner with no other noises interrupting us. I had one ear listening to the kids and the other listening for any tiny noise around the house. The constant vigilance was starting to wear on us.

After dinner, we settled the kids into bed. Rachel seemed particularly clingy, wanting to stay up a little longer, but I reassured her that everything was fine. Once they were asleep, Ted and I sat down in the living room to talk.

"I talked to Peter Raymond today," I began. "He confirmed that the Sipples have been experiencing similar issues. They've had tools go missing, a tractor tipped over, and even workers quitting because they're too scared to stay past dusk. Peter mentioned that his family believes in Yowies and that many clans live within the Pilliga."

Ted sighed, rubbing his temples. "I'm still not sure what to think. It sounds crazy, but everything points to something unusual going on. Did they happen to say how we get rid of these Yowies? What are we supposed to do? We don't have a gun, and who knows if that would fix the problem or make it worse!"

"No, unfortunately," I said. "Apparently, disturbing their territory can upset them, but we haven't done anything to the property since we've been here."

Ted nodded. "Yeah, I don't know, babe. This all seems ridiculous. I can't believe we moved here for a new start, and now this crazy stuff is going on. It feels like there's a cloud over the property. Does it feel like that to you too?"

"Yes!" I exclaimed. "I always feel like I'm being watched, and there's a heaviness here that I didn't notice the first time we came. I'm at a loss as to what we can do, hon."

Ted paused for a moment, looking more serious. "I'm supposed to go on another truck run tomorrow. Do you think I should postpone it?"

I shook my head. "No, we need the money, and it's only for three days. I can handle it. Just make sure to call and check in when you can."

Ted looked uncertain but finally agreed. "Alright but promise me you'll stay safe and keep an eye on everything."

"I promise," I said, squeezing his hand.

The night passed uneventfully, but the tension was clear. Every creak and rustle seemed amplified in the quiet house. I found myself checking the camera live feeds repeatedly, hoping not to see anything but fearing what I might find.

8

MONKEY FACE

Morning came, and Ted went out to check the back door. He found a small, dead possum lying on the ground, likely thrown with force to make such a loud noise. It was unsettling to think that someone—or something—had done this to send a message. The poor thing.

We cleaned up the mess before the kids could see it and went inside to get the kids ready for school.

As they were putting their back packs on, Rachel approached me and asked, "Mama, can you or Dad drop us off at the bus stop?" Her request was casual, but I sensed a hint of unease beneath her words.

Ted was preparing to leave for his truck run, but I asked him if he could drop the kids off at the end of the driveway before heading out. He agreed without hesitation. As they were about to leave, I kissed each of them goodbye, reassuring Rachel that everything would be fine. I watched as Ted and the kids drove off, feeling a mix of anxiety and determination. Once they were out of sight, I turned and went into the study, ready to face another day of trying to unravel the mystery that had cast a shadow over our new home.

It was only an hour later when I got a frantic call from the school, telling me that Rachel and James wanted to be picked up as soon as possible. I asked if they were sick, but the school nurse said no, they were just very upset and asked for me to come and get them. Worried, I jumped in the car and headed to their school.

When I got there, the kids were sitting together in the nurse's office. James had his arm around Rachel, his protective instincts kicking in. I knelt and asked them what was wrong, but they just cuddled me and asked if we could leave. I spoke briefly to the school administrator, who confirmed that nothing physically was wrong with them, but they were clearly distressed. With a worried heart, I got the kids into the car.

On the way home, the kids finally opened up about what had happened. Each morning while they waited at the bus stop at the end of the driveway, they started hearing noises in the bushes. It would only happen on the days we did not wait with them to get onto the bus. They never saw anything until today when James was kicking rocks around and heard a noise. He looked up and briefly saw a "monkey face" peering from behind the bushes and trees. It quickly withdrew when it saw him looking at it. Startled, James backed away and noticed Rachel standing there trembling. Thankfully, the bus came at that moment, and they hopped on quickly.

Listening to their story, a chill ran down my spine. The description of the "monkey face" and the noises matched the strange occurrences we had been experiencing around our property. I assured the kids that they were safe now and that Ted and I would figure out what was going on.

As we drove home, my mind raced with fear and determination. I had to protect my children and get to the bottom of this mystery.

Once home, I settled the kids with some snacks and their favourite TV show, hoping to distract them from the morning's events. I then went to the study, determined to find more information and devise a plan.

I decided it was time to take this seriously and consider all possibilities. I reviewed the morning's footage, searching for any signs of the creature James had described. While nothing definitive appeared, there was an unmistakable sense that something was lurking in the shadows of our property. Given the angles of our security cameras, it could have easily slipped through a gap unnoticed.

I called Ted, explaining what had happened and expressing my growing concern. He was just as worried but reassured me that we would get through this together. We discussed installing motion-activated lights to deter whatever was out there.

Next, I called around to local lawn clipping services, asking if anyone could come out today to trim the bushes near the bus stop. I had to pay extra for the short notice, but it was well worth it. The less area there was for anything to hide, the better. It would also make the kids feel safer, knowing nothing could sneak up on them at the bus stop.

By evening, I felt a bit more prepared, but the anxiety remained. The kids seemed calmer, but I knew the fear was still lingering. As I tucked them into bed, I promised them that we would keep them safe, no matter what.

9

MORE THAN ONE

That night, I couldn't sleep. With Ted not being there, I felt a lot more vulnerable. I must have checked the doors and windows about five times, feeling like I was on security patrol. Every noise, every creak of the house, made my heart race. I kept the camera live feed open on my phone, watching for any sign of movement.

I was starting to realize that this was taking over my life.

After a long and exhausting day, I finally managed to drift off to sleep, the events of the day swirling in my mind. The house was silent, save for the occasional creak of the old wood and the gentle hum of the wind outside. Just as I was about to slip into a deep sleep, a loud thump echoed from above, jolting me awake.

My heart pounded as I lay still, straining to hear over the thudding in my chest. At first, I tried to convince myself it was just a possum, but then I heard footsteps—heavy, deliberate footsteps—moving across the roof. The weight of them was far too much for any small animal. Each step seemed to reverberate through the house, sending chills down my spine.

I lay there, paralysed with fear, listening to the slow, methodical pacing above me. The footsteps moved from one end of the house to the other, as if something was surveying the entire roof. I glanced at the clock on my bedside table; it was just after 2 AM. Ted was on his truck run, and I was alone in the house with the kids. I had never felt so vulnerable in my life.

The noise stopped for a moment, and I dared to hope that whatever it was had left. But then there was another thump, closer this time, as if it had jumped to another part of the roof. I could hear the distinct sound of scraping, like claws or nails dragging across the shingles. The sound made my skin crawl.

I reached for my phone with trembling hands, keeping my eyes on the ceiling as if I could see through it to whatever was up there. I opened the camera app, flipping through the live feeds from the cameras Ted and I had set up. Nothing. The cameras showed only darkness and the faint outlines of trees swaying in the night breeze.

I switched to the camera facing the backyard, the one closest to the part of the roof where I last heard the noise. As I watched, I saw a shadow pass over the camera, too large and too quick to be an animal. I gasped, my breath catching in my throat. If one passed the camera that meant there was more than one out there.

My mind raced with thoughts of what to do. Should I go out there and confront it? Should I call the police? I didn't want to leave the kids alone, and I didn't want to make a noise that would draw attention to us. The footsteps started again, moving towards the edge of the roof above my bedroom.

I could hear the tiles creaking under the weight, and then, a loud thud as if something had jumped off the roof and landed on the ground below. My heart was in my throat as I switched back to the front door camera, hoping to catch a glimpse of whatever it was.

The camera caught the edge of a shadow moving quickly across the yard and disappearing behind the shed. I felt a moment of relief that they seemed to be gone, but the fear lingered that they would come back. The Yowies had been on my roof, and they had been close. Too close.

With my hands shaking, I dialed the local police station. The officer who answered sounded sleepy and somewhat annoyed, but I explained the situation as calmly as I could. They said they'd send someone out, but being a rural area, I knew it would take some time.

By the time the police arrived, the house was silent again.

Two officers knocked on the door, and I let them in, explaining what had happened. They walked around the property, shining their flashlights into the bushes and checking the roof. After about half an hour, they returned.

"There's nothing out there now," one of the officers said. "It's probably just a possum or a kangaroo. They can make quite a racket sometimes."

I nodded, not entirely convinced but grateful they had come. "Thank you for checking," I said.

"Just keep the doors and windows locked," the other officer advised. "And if it happens again, give us a call."

After they left, I lay back down, my body trembling, and stared at the ceiling. Sleep was out of the question now. I stayed awake, listening for any sound, any sign that it might return. The house was silent once more, but I knew I wouldn't feel safe until Ted was back, and we had a plan to deal with this.

10

NEIGHBOUR'S ENCOUNTERS

As the first light of dawn crept through the windows, I finally allowed myself to relax, but only a little. It was the weekend, and the kids were already up, watching something on Netflix and munching on their cereal.

I sat at the dining table, staring out the front window, feeling an overwhelming sense of weakness. It felt like we were being terrorised, and I had no idea why. Did they want to harm us, or were they just trying to drive us out? I couldn't make sense of it and felt utterly helpless. Snapping out of my thoughts, I told the kids we would go into town this morning. They cheered, and I knew it would be a good chance to take our minds off recent events.

We piled into the car and headed to town. As we passed the Sipples' property, I saw who I presumed to be Mr. Sipple walking the property with what looked like a hunting rifle. Telling myself that maybe he was shooting pests, I dared not think about what else might have been occurring there.

The kids and I enjoyed shopping and grabbed groceries for the week. Even though being at the house made me uncomfortable, I also felt like I needed to be there to protect it somehow. I worried when I was there, and I worried when I wasn't.

On the way home, I made a rash decision to stop at the Sipples' property and talk to Mr. Sipple.

I pulled into their driveway, my heart racing with a mix of anxiety and determination. I needed answers, and I hoped Mr. Sipple could provide some. As I stepped out of the car, he looked up from his inspection of the grounds, his rifle resting casually over his shoulder. I told the kids to stay in the car.

"Morning," I called out, walking towards him. "I'm Michelle, we just moved in down the road. Do you have a moment to talk?"

Mr. Sipple gave me a curt nod and motioned for me to join him on the porch. Up close, he was a rugged man in his late sixties, with a weathered tanned face and eyes that held a lifetime of stories.

"I've been meaning to introduce myself," I began, trying to keep my voice steady. "We've been having some… strange occurrences at our place. I saw a figure on our barn roof, loud noises at night, something through a dead possum at our house too. I was hoping you might have some insights."

Mr. Sipple's face darkened. "You're not the only ones. My property's been the same, maybe worse. Tools moved, machinery tipped over, workers quitting because they said they have seen things."

He paused, looking out over the fields, then continued, "I grew up in this area, you know. My family always believed in the Yowies. You know what Yowies are, right, Michelle?" he said, looking at me. "I never had any issues with them, though. Camped in the Pilliga plenty of times, never had a problem. But these ones... they're different. They're angry and seem to want to harm us. They terrorize my family almost every night."

A chill ran down my spine. "What do you think is causing this change in behaviour?"

Mr. Sipple shook his head. "I wish I knew. They never used to be this aggressive. It's like something has stirred them up, made them hostile. And it's not just random mischief. Lately I have been thinking they want to harm us. Hence the rifle sitting over there."

I felt a surge of fear and frustration. "So, what do we do? How do we protect our families?" We don't own a rifle.

He sighed deeply, his eyes meeting mine with a look of shared concern. "First thing is to stay vigilant. Keep your property well-lit at night. Have you got motion-activated? Those will help. They never step into the light. Maybe they don't want to be seen or their eyes are sensitive to it. Who knows? Also, keep your cameras rolling. Document everything. The more evidence we have, the better we can understand what's going on."

I nodded, absorbing his advice. "Thank you, Mr. Sipple. It's reassuring to know we're not alone in this. But it's also terrifying to think about what we might be dealing with."

He gave a small, grim smile. "You're welcome. And call me Frank. We're neighbours, after all. Just remember, the Yowies I've known were more curious than harmful. But these... these are different. Be careful, and don't hesitate to reach out if you need anything." He handed me a slip of paper with his phone number. "I will come straight away with my rifle."

I thanked him again and headed back to the car, my mind

racing with new information and fresh fears. As I drove home, I couldn't shake the feeling that our situation was far more dangerous than I had realised. We were not just dealing with mysterious creatures; we were dealing with something angry and vengeful.

What these Yowies were was beyond my understanding. I figured they were flesh and blood, but like the First Nations people (and others) believed, they existed in both the spirit world and our world. How do we combat the enemy when we do not understand exactly what the enemy is? I was lost and way out of my depth. My mind wasn't on work, and I seemed to be in a daze half the time. I was completely overwhelmed with the situation.

11

THE OPEN DOOR

As we drove up the driveway to our home, a sense of relief began to wash over me. The outing had done us some good, a brief respite from the tension that had been building. The kids were chatting excitedly about the new snacks we had bought and the movies they wanted to watch that night. For a moment, everything felt normal.

But as we got closer to the house, my heart suddenly sank. The front door was open. I was positive I had closed and locked it before we left.

"Mama, why is the door open?" James asked, his voice tinged with confusion.

I forced a smile, trying to keep my voice steady. "I'm sure it's nothing, sweetheart. You two stay in the car for a moment, okay?"

I parked the car and turned off the engine, my mind racing. After telling the kids to stay put, I took a deep breath and stepped out. The afternoon sun cast long shadows, and a cold wind blew, prompting me to pull my cardigan tight around me. As I walked up the porch, that familiar stench hit me. The foul, heavy smell was unmistakable—like rotting meat and garbage. My stomach churned, and I tried to steady myself.

"Mama, do you smell that?" Rachel called out from the car; her nose wrinkled in disgust.

"Yes, honey. Just stay in the car," I replied, trying to mask my own unease.

The house was eerily silent as I approached the open door. The wind rustled the leaves, and the creak of the porch floorboards echoed in the stillness. I peered into the house, half-expecting to see some sign of intrusion, but everything seemed undisturbed. Curiously, the smell wasn't inside.

"Hello?" I called out, my voice barely above a whisper. There was no answer.

Steeling myself, I stepped inside. The living room was empty, everything in its place. I moved cautiously from room to room, checking for any signs of disturbance. The kitchen was as we had left it, and the dining room was untouched. But as I reached the hallway leading to the bedrooms, a sense of unease settled over me.

The door to the kids' room was ajar. I pushed it open, holding my breath. The room was empty, the beds neatly made. I let out a sigh of relief but couldn't shake the feeling that something was off. I checked my bedroom and the bathroom, but everything seemed normal.

Returning to the living room, I noticed the back door was still locked. I double-checked the windows, all securely shut. I couldn't find any sign of forced entry, but when I went back to the front door, I saw it—the lock had been busted. It wasn't the wind that had opened the door; someone or something had broken in.

I walked back to the car, my heart still racing. The kids looked at me expectantly, and I forced another smile.

"Everything's fine," I lied. "Must have been the wind or something. Come on, let's get inside."

James and Rachel hesitated for a moment before following me out of the car. I kept a close watch on them as we made our way into the house, every sense on high alert. Once we were inside, I asked the kids to go play in their rooms while I called a local locksmith. There was only one in town, and once again I had to pay a small fortune to get them to come out within the hour. Thankfully, they did, and the kids were unaware as they stayed in their rooms. The door wasn't structurally damaged, just the lock, thankfully.

With the kids still playing in their bedrooms, I busied myself in the kitchen, trying to shake off the unease. But the image of the open door and the busted lock stayed with me.

I don't think whatever it had come into the house, as the smell was only concentrated outside on the porch. That means it just broke the door lock to let us know it could, or did it hear us coming down the road and we interrupted its plan? Obviously, I would never find out the truth, but either way, those scenarios made me nauseous.

12

PANIC ATTACK

After dinner, the kids played in their bedroom, seemingly moving on from the earlier experience. I sat down at my desk and tried to get as much work done as possible. If I didn't work, I didn't get paid after all.

The hours slipped by, and it was about 10 PM when I realised, I had forgotten to put the kids to bed. I went into their rooms and found them already sound asleep. Feeling bad that I hadn't checked on them sooner, I walked back out to make a coffee.

Not wanting to stop working, I made my coffee extra strong and headed back to the study.

The house was quiet, the soft hum of the refrigerator the only background noise. I tried to focus on my work, but my mind kept drifting back to the open door and the broken lock. Was the Yowie sending us a message?

It was about an hour later when I started hearing a scratching noise. I stopped tapping away on the keyboard and sat back in my chair to listen. The sound was faint at first, almost like a whisper. I couldn't pinpoint where it was coming from, but it alternated between a rubbing sound and then a scratching sound.

My heart began to race as I strained to listen. The scratching grew louder, more insistent. I checked the camera feeds on my phone, but everything seemed normal outside. The kids were still asleep, and there was no sign of movement in the house.

The noise persisted, and it was starting to drive me crazy. I got up from my desk and walked around the house, trying to locate the source. As I moved through the hallway, the sound seemed to follow me, echoing through the walls. I checked the doors and windows again, making sure everything was secure.

Returning to the study, I sat down and listened intently. The scratching was still there, almost as if it was right below me. I glanced down at the floor, the realisation dawning on me. The noise was coming from under the house, right below where I sat.

My blood ran cold. What could be down there? I debated whether to investigate or wake the kids and leave the house. The thought of facing whatever was making that noise alone terrified me, but the idea of putting the kids at risk was even worse.

Gathering my courage, I grabbed a flashlight and headed to the back door. I was absolutely terrified, but I was tired of not knowing for sure what we were dealing with. I needed to see what was under the house, but I couldn't shake the feeling that I was making a terrible mistake. It felt like one of those moments in a horror movie where you scream at the foolish person not to go outside. Yeah, I was the foolish person.

I stepped outside, the cool night air biting at my skin. The backyard was eerily silent. There was little help from the moon, but my flashlight provided just enough light to see by. I took a deep breath and started toward the shadowy area under the house, my flashlight beam cutting through the darkness.

I slowly walked down the back steps, half-expecting a hand to reach out from under them. I walked out onto the grass and could see under the house but not very far. If I was going to see what was under the study area, I would have to get down low. I forced myself to walk around the side of the house, staying about three metres away from it. I reached the study, took a deep breath, and got down on my knees. I couldn't hear any sounds, so I pointed the flashlight at the area under the study and waved it slowly from side to side slowly. There was nothing there.

A low growl emanated from the darkness behind me, and my heart sank. *You've got to be shitting me*, I thought. The freaking thing was behind me. I slowly got to my feet and turned around, pointing the flashlight in the direction of the growl. There was a White Cypress Pine about 25 to 30 metres away that had fallen many years ago. With my hands shaking, I pointed the light towards the old tree and saw two glowing amber eyes, as large as baseballs, at least eight feet off the ground. I could just make out a dark silhouette that was unbelievably massive.

I froze, but I knew I had to get back inside and secure the house. I forced myself to take a step toward the back of the house, then walked back slowly, keeping the light on the Yowie. I forced myself to turn and walk up the stairs slowly and secured the door behind me. That thing could have easily busted through the door, but I felt a little safer being inside.

My hands were shaking, and I could barely catch my breath. I checked on the kids one more time, ensuring they were safe and sound. Despite this, I still couldn't catch my breath and started hyperventilating. I sat down in the hallway, my chest tight, feeling dizzy and out of control. My heart was pounding, and I felt an overwhelming sense of dread. I was having what I now know was a panic attack.

I tried to get my breathing under control, inhaling through my nose and exhaling through my mouth. Gradually, I could feel my body start to relax. The tightness in my chest eased, and the dizziness began to fade. Eventually, I felt my heart rate slow down, and I got up slowly and walked into the study.

13

HOWLS

Sitting back at my desk, I tried to make sense of what had just happened. I had seen deer, foxes, and canine eye shine but never amber eye shine. And certainly not *that* big. It was like the eyes were back lit or something.

And the size of its body thing! If its eyes were eight feet off the ground, then it stood at least 8.5 to 9 feet tall. From what I could tell, even though it was massive, it had a kind of V shape—very wide at the shoulders and tapered in at the waist. Its hands nearly reached its knees. I couldn't see any further past the knee area due to the brush and I couldn't see its face very well, although its head was kind of cone-shaped, but not overly so *(see the cover image—Luka did a brilliant job of capturing our description)*. It didn't seem to move at all either, just like a statue.

Then it occurred to me: it had the opportunity to sneak up on me and kill me. Why didn't it take the chance? The thought was both chilling and oddly comforting. Perhaps it wasn't purely malevolent.

I called Ted and caught him up to speed. He was annoyed at me that I went outside but understood why I had to know what it was. He would be home tomorrow afternoon and for that I was grateful. I always felt safer with him around.

I did my nightly security check around the house, ensuring all doors and windows were locked tight. The kids were sound asleep, and I felt a pang of guilt for the fear they must have been feeling. I hoped a good night's rest would ease their worries, if only for a little while.

After my rounds, I headed to bed and put on an episode of Suits on the iPad, trying to concentrate on the charming Harvey Specter. His confident smirk and quick wit were a welcome distraction from the anxiety that had settled deep within me. Eventually, exhaustion took over, and I drifted off to sleep.

A few hours later, I was jolted awake by a noise outside. It started as a low, guttural growl, unmistakably close. My heart raced as I lay still, trying to make sense of what I was hearing. The growl grew louder, morphing into a deep, resonant howl that sent shivers down my spine.

I crept out of bed and moved silently to the window, peeking through the curtains. The moonlight cast an eerie glow over the yard, but I couldn't see anything unusual. I strained my ears, listening intently.

The howling continued, echoing through the still night air. It was a sound like the ones I had heard on YouTube—the calls and screams attributed to Bigfoot.

Just as I thought it couldn't get any worse, the single howl was joined by another, then another. Soon, the night was filled with the unmistakable calls of at least three Yowies, each one distinct but equally terrifying. The hairs on the back of my neck stood up as the realisation hit me: they were communicating with each other.

The calls were a mix of howls, grunts, and whoops, each one more chilling than the last. It was as if they were surrounding the house, closing in on us. I felt a wave of panic wash over me, but I forced myself to stay calm. I had to protect my family and the last thing I needed was another panic attack.

I grabbed my phone from my bedside table and quietly made my way to the kids' rooms. Rachel and James were still asleep, thankfully oblivious to the terrifying sounds outside. I checked the locks on their windows once more, reassuring myself that they were secure.

I returned to the living room and glanced at the live camera feed on my phone. The cameras showed nothing but darkness and the occasional sway of the trees in the breeze. The Yowies were out there, but they were staying out of sight.

As I peered out the window, I noticed shadows moving just beyond the reach of the outside lights. It was as if they knew exactly where to stand to avoid being seen. The realisation that they were aware of our security measures and were deliberately staying out of sight made my blood run cold. They were intelligent.

The howls grew louder, more insistent. I couldn't ignore the feeling that they were trying to lure me outside, to draw me into the darkness where they held the advantage. My mind raced with questions. What did they want? Why were they here? And most importantly, how could I protect my family from something so powerful and unknown?

I picked up my phone and dialed Ted's number. He answered, his voice filled with concern as I explained what was happening. "Stay inside and keep the doors locked," he advised. "I'll be home as quick I can."

Hanging up, I felt a mixture of relief and dread. Ted's presence would be comforting, but he was hours away, and the Yowies were here now.

I paced the living room, keeping an eye on the camera live feed and listening to the unnerving chorus outside. The calls continued for what felt like an eternity, each one a reminder of the danger lurking just beyond the safety of our walls.

Eventually, the howls began to fade, and the night grew quiet once more. I stayed vigilant, unable to shake the feeling that this was just the beginning. The Yowies had made their presence known, and their message was clear: we were not alone.

As dawn approached, I finally allowed myself to sit down, exhausted but resolute. We can't keep doing this, I thought.

14

GETTING BOLDER

The kids woke up, and soon the house was filled with laughing, arguing, and the Disney Kids channel. At least they weren't showing any worries, and I was sure if they had heard anything last night, they would have mentioned it.

Ted got home a few hours early, his face etched with concern as I recounted the events of the previous night. He listened intently, his brow furrowing deeper with each detail. "We can't keep living like this," he said finally. "We need to take more measures to secure the house."

After our discussion, Ted insisted that I take a nap while he watched the kids. Exhaustion hit me as soon as my head hit the pillow, and I was grateful for the chance to rest, even if it was just for a short while.

Ted kept the kids entertained with a game of Uno, their laughter a welcome distraction from the fear that had gripped us. Once I woke up, feeling slightly more refreshed, we decided to go into town to get more lights and cameras. The more we could do to protect our home, the better.

The trip to town was a mix of normalcy and urgency. We picked up additional security lights and cameras, and Ted even bought a few extra locks for the doors and windows. The kids enjoyed the outing, blissfully unaware of the real reason behind our shopping spree.

Back home, Ted and I spent the afternoon setting up the new equipment. The extra lights would cover the blind spots around the house, and the cameras would provide a clearer view of the property. As we worked, I felt a glimmer of hope that these measures might give us some peace of mind.

As evening approached, the house felt more secure than it had in days. The new lights cast a comforting glow over the yard, and the cameras were strategically placed to catch any movement. Ted and I double-checked everything, making sure there were no gaps in our defenses.

That night, after dinner, we gathered in the living room to watch a movie. The kids were excited about the new setup and eager to test out the cameras. Ted showed them how to check the live camera feed on the app, and they took turns looking for any signs of movement outside.

The movie ended, and we put the kids to bed. I could tell they were a bit apprehensive, but Ted's presence seemed to reassure them. Once they were asleep, we sat together in the living room, keeping a watchful eye on the camera live feeds.

Around midnight, the familiar sounds of the Australian bush began to change. The usual chirping of crickets and rustling of leaves gave way to an eerie silence. Ted and I exchanged a worried glance, and I felt a familiar knot of fear tightening in my stomach.

Suddenly, the camera app picked up movement near the edge of the property. We leaned in closer, trying to make out what it was. A shadowy figure moved just beyond the reach of the lights, staying in the darkness. It was too large to be an animal, and my heart sank as I realized it was one of the Yowies.

The figure stayed there for a few minutes, seemingly watching the house. Ted and I held our breath, waiting for it to make a move. Then, as suddenly as it had appeared, it slipped back into the darkness.

Ted's face was pale as he turned to me. "They're getting bolder," he said quietly. "We need to stay on high alert."

I nodded, fear gripping me once again. "We'll get through this," I said, more to reassure myself than him. I was glad though that Ted had seen that there was something out there. It reassured me that I hadn't gone completely nuts.

The rest of the night passed uneventfully, but neither of us could sleep. We took turns watching the camera app, ready to respond to any sign of danger. The Yowies were out there, and we had to be ready for whatever came next.

As dawn broke, I felt a mix of relief and dread. The night had passed without incident, but it was evident we were not alone. The Yowies were watching, waiting.

15

ROCK THROWING

It was a Monday, so I went through the usual morning ritual of making breakfast for the kids, reminding them to brush their teeth, and getting them ready for school. Ted, sensing my exhaustion, offered to walk them down to the bus stop while I jumped in the shower. I was grateful for the small reprieve and relished the thought of hot water washing away the remnants of last night's tension.

As the steam filled the bathroom, I tried to clear my mind. The Yowies were becoming more aggressive, and the thought of them lurking just beyond our property sent chills down my spine. But for now, I focused on the warmth of the shower and the brief moment of privacy.

I was just about finished when Ted burst through the bathroom door, flustered and out of breath. "The damn thing threw rocks at me," he exclaimed, his eyes wide with alarm.

"What?" I asked, turning off the water and grabbing a towel. "Are you serious?"

"Dead serious," Ted panted, leaning against the sink. "I got the kids on the bus, and as I was walking back, I heard something rustling in the bushes, you know, behind where I park my truck."

I wrapped the towel around me and stepped closer, concern creeping into my voice. "What did you see?"

Ted took a deep breath, his eyes wide. "At first, I didn't see anything. I just heard the rustling. Then, out of nowhere, a rock landed right in front of me. It wasn't just a small pebble; it was a good-sized rock. I stopped and looked in the direction it had come from, but there was nothing. No movement, no sound."

My stomach was in knots listening to Ted. He wasn't one to get spooked easily. "Did you see anyone or anything?"

He shook his head. "No, nothing. But as I started walking again, feeling a little anxious, I heard this almighty scream coming from those bushes. It sounded like a woman being skinned alive. It was so loud, and it felt like it shook my bones. I just took off running back to the house."

Did the Yowie mean to hit Ted, or was it just trying to let him know it was there? We discussed this as I went into the bedroom to get dressed. There was nothing else we could do for defense. We didn't have a gun, and I doubted a kitchen knife would do more than annoy them. We felt so helpless.

Ted had to go into town to run some errands and asked if I wanted to go with him. I declined, saying I needed to do some laundry and get some work done while the kids were at school.

I watched him drive down the long driveway, hoping all would be quiet while he was gone.

16

DAMNED IF YOU DO

A few hours later, Ted came back from town with a different kind of energy, his face a mix of excitement and concern.

"Hey hon. "I talked to some people in town. They had some interesting things to say about the Yowies, he said."

I looked up from my laptop, curiosity piqued. "What did they say?"

Ted sat down, rubbing the back of his neck. "Well, besides the few that laughed at me, opinions were all over the place. One guy suggested that we should put out an offering, like fruits or vegetables, at the edge of the forest. He said it might help keep them calm, kind of like a peace gesture."

I raised an eyebrow. "And the others?"

Ted sighed. "Another guy was adamant that we'd regret doing that. He said offering food could make things worse, make them more aggressive or dependent on us. He basically told me not to mess with them at all."

My heart sank. "So, what do we do? It sounds like there's no clear answer."

Ted shook his head, frustration evident on his face. "I know. It's like a damned if you do, damned if you don't situation. But we must do something. We can't keep living like this."

I leaned back in my chair, processing everything. "Maybe we should try the offering. If it doesn't work or if it makes things worse, we can always stop. At least we'll be doing something proactive."

Ted nodded slowly, his expression serious. "Okay, let's start there. I'll get some fruits and vegetables and set them out tonight."

17

THE OFFERING

The rest of the day passed in a blur of activity. Ted worked on the truck and installed the new security measures, while I tried to focus on my work, my mind constantly drifting back to the Yowies and what lay ahead.

In the late afternoon, Ted walked down to meet the kids when they got off the bus, making sure they were safe and trying to act normal despite the underlying tension.

As night fell, we sat together in the living room, going over our plan.

"Do you think this will work?" I asked, my voice barely above a whisper.

"I hope so," Ted replied, squeezing my hand. "At least we're trying something."

As we prepared the first offering, setting a basket of fruits and vegetables right next to the shed, a sense of unease lingered in the air. We returned to the house, locking the doors and windows, and sat in the living room, the tension intense.

"Do you think they'll come tonight?" I asked quietly.

Ted shrugged. "I don't know. But whatever happens, we're ready."

The kids now in bed, we sat in silence, listening to the night sounds, hoping our gesture would be enough to keep the Yowies at bay and bring some peace to our troubled lives. The cameras and lights were in place, and we watched the live feed on my phone, waiting for any sign of movement.

Hours passed, and the night remained quiet. Just as we were beginning to relax, a movement on one of the feeds caught our attention. A dark figure slowly peaked from behind the corner of the shed where we had placed the offering. We held our breath, watching intently.

The figure bent down, seemingly inspecting the basket. It moved slowly, cautiously, as if unsure what to make of the gesture. Then, it disappeared back behind the shed, leaving the offering untouched.

Ted and I exchanged a glance, a mix of relief and apprehension. "Well, I guess it didn't like our offering," I said softly.

"Yeah," Ted agreed. "But it just might have been cautious and will come back later for it."

We sat back, still on edge but hopeful that our gesture might lead to a peaceful resolution. As the night wore on, we kept a close watch on the live camera feed, ready for whatever came next.

18

THAT DIDN'T GO TO PLAN

We were sitting quietly, each on our phones, trying to distract ourselves from the anxiety that had settled over the house. The soft glow of our screens was the only light in the room when suddenly, we heard a loud thud. We both looked at each other, wide-eyed.

Before we could process it, another thud echoed through the house. Suddenly, there was noise everywhere—thuds, cracks, and a strange, almost rhythmic pounding.

I quickly brought up the camera live feed on my phone, my heart racing. Three out of the seven cameras we had installed were blank. "What the heck is going on?" I muttered, frantically switching between the remaining live feeds.

Ted leaned over to look at my screen, his expression a mix of confusion and fear. "Why are the cameras down?"

Then it hit me. "Ted, they're throwing the apples we left them at the lights and cameras!"

Ted's eyes widened in realisation. "They're trying to blind us, make it so we can't see them."

I switched to the front camera feed just in time to see a large apple smash into the lens, the feed going black immediately. "They're smart," I said, my voice trembling. "Too smart."

Ted jumped up and headed down the hall. "We need to check on the kids, make sure they're safe."

We hurried down the hall, the thudding and crashing continuing outside. We quietly opened the door to the kids' room. They were fast asleep, undisturbed by the chaos outside. I felt a small wave of relief wash over me as I watched their peaceful faces.

"They're okay," I whispered to Ted. "Let's go back to the living room."

We returned to the living room, the noise outside still raging. The sound of glass shattering came from the backyard. "That was the porch light," I whispered to Ted. "They're getting bolder."

Ted nodded grimly. "We need to stay calm and think this through. We can't let them know we're scared."

We sat back down, the iPhones in our hands providing a small circle of light in the otherwise dark room. The noise continued for what felt like hours, each crash and thud making us flinch. We kept our eyes on the remaining camera feeds, watching for any sign that the Yowies were trying to enter the house.

Suddenly, I looked up at the living room window and saw the silhouette of a Yowie. I gasped, and Ted followed my gaze, whispering, "Don't move." We sat frozen, holding our breath, as the Yowie stood there for what felt like an eternity. After a minute, it turned and disappeared into the shadows. It was showing us it was intelligent: the camera feed above the window was now dead.

Eventually, the noise began to subside. The thudding and crashing grew less frequent until, finally, there was silence. Ted and I exchanged wary glances, unsure if the ordeal was truly over.

"Do you think they're gone?" I whispered.

Ted nodded slowly. "Maybe. But let's wait a bit longer to be sure."

As dawn approached, we cautiously made our way around the house, checking the windows and doors. The outside of the house was a mess—broken lights, shattered glass, and debris everywhere. But it seemed the Yowies had retreated, at least for now.

"We need to clean this up and figure out our next move," Ted said, surveying the damage. "Clearly they didn't appreciate our offering basket."

I nodded, feeling a mix of exhaustion and determination. "We'll get through this," I said, looking around at the wreckage. "We have to."

As we began to clean up the aftermath of the night, one thing was clear: the Yowies were getting more aggressive, and we needed to find a way to protect our home or just pack up and leave.

19

CUNNING BASTARDS

The next morning, despite the chaos of the night, we tried to maintain a sense of normalcy for the kids. They woke up, unaware of the night's events, and got ready for school as usual. Over breakfast, we kept the conversation light, talking about their upcoming day and their friends. Ted walked them to the bus stop, making sure they were safe and settled before it drove off.

Once the kids were on their way, we turned our attention to the house. Ted and I started replacing the broken light bulbs around the exterior. The damage was worse than we'd initially thought; several cameras were broken beyond repair, their lenses cracked, and their wiring exposed. The ones that were still intact just needed a good cleaning to remove the remnants of smashed apples and mud.

"I can't believe they targeted the cameras and lights so precisely," I said, wiping a smudge off a camera lens. "They're smarter than we gave them credit for."

Ted nodded; his jaw set in determination. "We need to be

smarter too. This isn't just about scaring them off anymore. It's about protecting our home."

With the immediate repairs done, we decided to pay a visit to Frank Sipple, one of our neighbours who lived a few miles down the road. Ted knew I had spoken to Frank about our ongoing Yowie issues and we hoped he would have some more answers for us.

We drove down the dirt road to Frank's house, the morning sun casting long shadows across the forest. As we pulled up, Frank was outside, tending to a patch of vegetables.

"Morning, Frank," I called out as we got out of the car.

Frank looked up, a curious expression on his face. "Morning, Michelle. You look like you've seen a ghost."

"Something like that," I replied and introduced Ted to Frank. "Mind if we talk for a bit?" I asked.

"Sure, come on in," Frank said, leading us into the house.

Inside, the house was modern and well-organised. We sat down at the kitchen table, and Frank poured us some coffee.

"Have you had more things happen on your property?" Frank asked, sitting down across from us.

Ted and I took turns explaining the events of the past few nights—the sightings, the noises, the attack on our cameras and lights. Frank listened intently, his brow furrowing deeper with each detail.

"That doesn't sound good, guys. To me, it sounds like they're escalating, right?"

"Yeah, it seems so," said Ted.

Frank leaned back in his chair, a grim look on his face. "Well, we had an incident two nights ago too. It had been quiet for a few days, and then the banging on the house started. Next thing you know, a wheelbarrow that one of the workers must have left out gets thrown into the side of my work truck. I was livid, so without thinking, I grabbed my rifle and shot at it from the front porch. No idea if I actually hit it, but if they come back, I will keep on shooting at them. I am tired of it. My wife is threatening to take the kids to her mother's if it doesn't get sorted in the next couple of days."

Ted and I exchanged worried glances. "We need to come up with a plan," Ted said. "We can't keep living like this. And shooting at them might just make things worse."

Frank nodded, though he didn't look entirely convinced. "I hear you, but what else can we do? These things are relentless. And they are cunning bastards."

"We need to find a way to protect our homes without provoking them further," I suggested. "Maybe we can pool our resources and come up with a solution together. More lights, better cameras, maybe even some deterrents that won't escalate the situation."

Frank sighed. "I hope you're right. But we need to act fast. My wife is serious about leaving, and I can't blame her. This is no way to live."

As we finished our coffee, we discussed possible strategies. We agreed to stay in close contact and to inform each other of any new incidents immediately. Frank mentioned he had some old contacts who might know more about dealing with Yowies, and he promised to reach out to them.

"I'd tell you guys to get a gun, but they are not so easy to apply for and lord knows it takes forever to get approved, even when you live on rural property," Frank said as we stood to leave. "Yeah, I had thought of that too, replied Ted."

First Lesson: Bronze casting sculpture by Brett Garling looking over the Dandry Gorge as part of Sculptures in the Scrub in the heart of the Pilliga Forest - near Baradine, New South Wales. Photo by Vivian Evans.

20

BLOOD RUNS COLD

As we drove back home from Frank's house, the weight of the situation pressed heavily on our minds. Ted and I exchanged a few words about the conversation with Frank, but mostly, we drove in silence, lost in our thoughts.

When we reached home, it was nearly time for the kids to get off the bus. We parked the car near the house and started walking down our driveway to meet the kids at the bus stop. The late afternoon sun cast long shadows, and the familiar crunch of gravel under our feet was a small comfort amidst our growing anxiety.

As we walked, Ted suddenly reached out his hand to stop me. I looked at him, confused. "What's the matter?" I asked in a hushed tone.

He motioned with his head towards the edge of the scrub. I followed his gaze and felt my blood run cold. Standing just at the edge of the scrub was a Yowie. It was watching us, its eyes reflecting a knowing look, as if it understood our fear.

Shaking, I whispered to Ted, "What should we do?"

Before he could answer, the Yowie turned and disappeared into the bush, moving with a grace that belied its size. We stood there for a moment, stunned and unsure of what to do next. The terror was so intense that my whole body felt paralysed.

"Let's keep moving," Ted said finally, his voice steady but tense. "We need to get the kids."

With each step, I had to will my legs to cooperate, my mind screaming for me to turn and run back to the house. We resumed our walk down the driveway, our eyes darting to the spot where the Yowie had stood. By the time we reached the bus stop, the kids were already getting off the bus, their faces lighting up when they saw us.

"Hey, kids!" I called out, forcing a smile as they ran towards us.

"Mama! Dad!" they chorused, their excitement a brief respite from our fear.

We exchanged hugs and walked back to the house together, the kids chattering excitedly about their day at school. Ted and I kept glancing at the edge of the scrub, our senses on high alert. The kids, blissfully unaware, continued their stories, their laughter a stark contrast to the tension we felt.

Once inside, the kids settled at the kitchen table with their homework. I helped them with their assignments, while Ted sat down on his favourite recliner and read the news on his phone. The familiar routine was a welcome distraction, and for a little while, we managed to push thoughts of the Yowies to the back of our minds.

I joined him in the living room after the kids were done with their homework. A few minutes to relax before starting dinner.

As dusk approached, the kids were watching TV, blissfully unaware of the tension that gripped us. I started preparing dinner, trying to focus on the simple tasks of chopping vegetables and stirring pots. The mundane routine helped calm my nerves, but the underlying fear never completely went away.

After dinner, we put the kids to bed, making sure to lock their windows and draw the curtains tightly. Ted and I exchanged a glance as we tucked them in, silently reassuring each other that we would do everything possible to keep them safe.

We retreated to the living room; our phones close at hand. The camera app displayed the feeds from the remaining functional cameras, and we watched them intently, waiting for any sign of movement.

"Do you think they'll come back tonight?" I asked, my voice barely above a whisper.

Ted sighed, running a hand through his hair. "I don't know. But we have to be ready for anything."

The hours passed slowly, the silence only broken by the occasional creak of the house settling or the distant call of a night bird. Every so often, we exchanged worried glances, but mostly, we sat in tense silence, our eyes glued to our phones.

Just as we began to relax, we heard heavy, deliberate footfalls outside the living room. They were slow and methodical, each step sending a chill down my spine. Ted and I exchanged a glance, fear evident in both our eyes.

"Do you hear that?" I whispered, my voice trembling.

"Yeah," Ted replied, his jaw clenched. "They're right outside."

We listened intently, the footfalls continuing their ominous march around the house. They paused occasionally, as if the Yowie was inspecting the perimeter, searching for a way in.

"What should we do?" I asked, gripping Ted's arm tightly.

"Stay quiet," he whispered back. "Let's see what they do."

The footfalls moved closer, stopping just outside the living room window. We held our breath, the tension almost unbearable. Then, just as suddenly as they had started, the footsteps receded, disappearing into the night.

Ted let out a shaky breath. "They're testing us," he said, his voice barely audible. "Seeing how far they can push us and one thing for sure, they know exactly where the cameras are."

21

STAY QUIET

....

The night stretched on, and despite our vigilance, exhaustion began to take its toll. The tension of the day, coupled with the fear of the Yowies' presence, had worn us down. Ted and I exchanged tired glances, knowing we needed rest to face whatever challenges lay ahead.

"We should try to get some sleep," Ted said softly, his eyes heavy with fatigue. "We'll need our strength for tomorrow."

I nodded, though the thought of closing my eyes and letting down our guard made my stomach churn with anxiety. Still, we had no choice. We couldn't keep going like this without some rest.

We checked the live feed one last time, then reluctantly headed to bed. As we lay down, the darkness of the room seemed to press in on us, amplifying every creak and rustle outside. I could feel my heart pounding in my chest, but exhaustion soon began to pull me towards sleep.

Just as we were starting to drift off, about ten minutes after laying down, we heard the footfalls again. My eyes snapped open, and I could see Ted was already alert, listening intently. The heavy, deliberate steps echoed outside our bedroom, each one resonating through the floorboards.

"Do you hear that?" I whispered, my voice trembling.

Ted nodded; his jaw clenched. "Yeah. They're right outside."

The footsteps were closer this time, louder and more menacing. We could hear the Yowie's breathing, deep and heavy, as if it were right on the other side of the wall. The sound sent chills down my spine, and I was amazed at how big it must have been for us to hear it so clearly.

We lay there, frozen in fear, listening to the creature's laboured breaths. It moved slowly around the outside of the house, its steps methodical and purposeful. I could feel the weight of its presence, each footfall making my heart race faster.

"What do we do?" I whispered, barely able to get the words out.

"Stay quiet," Ted replied, his voice tense. "Let's see if it leaves."

The Yowie's footsteps stopped right outside our bedroom window. We held our breath, the tension almost unbearable. The sound of its breathing was so close, I could almost feel the vibrations in the air. It stood there for what felt like an eternity, as if it knew we were inside, terrified and vulnerable.

Finally, after what seemed like hours, the footsteps began to move away. We listened as they receded into the distance, the breathing growing fainter until it was gone. Only then did we dare to exhale, the tension slowly ebbing away.

Ted let out a shaky breath. "They enjoy scaring us."

Tears started streaming down my face, the constant fear overwhelming me. Ted reached out and pulled me close, trying to console me. "We'll get through this," he whispered, his voice steady but strained.

I nodded, still too scared to speak. The reality of our situation was sinking in, and I knew we couldn't keep living like this. Something had to change.

We lay there in silence for a while longer, listening for any signs of the Yowie's return. When it seemed safe, we finally allowed ourselves to relax, though sleep was still elusive.

22

SCREAMING IN TERROR

The next few days passed without incident, but we didn't dare think the Yowies had gone away. The uneasy peace felt more like a temporary reprieve, a pause before the next inevitable encounter. We moved through our routines with an underlying sense of dread, constantly on edge and listening for any sign of their return. The quiet was unnerving, like the calm before a storm, and we knew better than to let our guard down.

Saturday night arrived, bringing with it a cold snap that signaled winter was well and truly here. Ted lit a fire in the fireplace, the crackling flames providing a comforting warmth and a sense of normalcy. The kids were excited to watch "Jumanji," a family favourite, and we all settled in the living room, trying to relax.

The movie played on, and for a little while, we were able to lose ourselves in the adventure on the screen. The sound of the wind outside was muted by the cozy interior, and the flickering fire cast dancing shadows on the walls. I almost dared to hope that things were returning to normal.

Suddenly, we heard a soft thump on the roof. Ted and I immediately looked up; our senses heightened by the unexpected noise. The kids were engrossed in the movie, but we exchanged a worried glance, our previous fears rushing back.

We both stared at the ceiling, trying to discern what could have made that sound. The thump had been soft, almost cautious, as if something—or someone—was testing the stability of the roof.

Then, without warning, the room erupted into chaos. There was a loud, crashing noise as something came hurtling down the chimney. The fire sputtered and flared, and in an instant, a large rock landed with a heavy thud on the hearth, sending embers and ash flying.

The kids screamed in terror, jumping up from the couch and hiding behind me. I instinctively pulled them close, trying to shield them from the debris. Ted sprang into action, stomping out the embers that had scattered across the floor. I grabbed a towel and quickly put out the embers that had blown up onto the couch where we had been sitting quietly just moments before.

"Get behind the couch!" Ted shouted, his voice a mix of fear and determination.

We huddled together on the floor behind the couch, the kids crying and clutching at us. The rock that had come down the chimney was massive, almost too large to have fit through the narrow passage. It was a deliberate act, a message from the Yowies that they were still here and more aggressive than ever.

"Dad, what was that?" James asked, his voice trembling.

Ted shot me a quick glance, his expression softening for a

moment. "A brick must have fallen off the chimney," he said, trying to keep his voice calm and steady. "Nothing to worry about. We're safe."

The kids seemed somewhat reassured, but their fear was still evident. Ted then grabbed the fire extinguisher and finished putting out any remaining embers, ensuring the fire was completely out. The acrid smell of smoke and the dying embers of the fire filled the room.

Minutes felt like hours as we stayed on high alert, waiting for the next move. But nothing else happened. The thumping on the roof ceased, and the night outside returned to its eerie stillness.

Finally, Ted put down the fire extinguisher, though his stance remained tense. "I think they're gone," he mouthed to me. "For now."

We slowly got up, the kids still clinging to us. Ted and I exchanged a look, knowing that this was far from over.

"Let's get the kids to bed," I suggested, trying to maintain some semblance of normalcy.

Ted nodded; his face set in a grim expression. "Yeah. Good idea.

As we tucked the kids into bed, their earlier excitement replaced by a sombre mood, I couldn't shake the feeling of dread that hung over us. The Yowies had made their presence known in a terrifying way, and we had no idea what they would do next.

We stayed up late that night, discussing our options and trying to come up with a plan. Without the fire going the cold air had crept in so we turned up the heaters—a stark reminder of the chilling presence just outside our walls.

One thing was clear: we couldn't keep living in fear. We couldn't put up with this any longer, and we were deeply worried for the kids. What if the fire had gotten out of control? Were they trying to force us outside?

23

A FEW DAYS REPRIEVE

The next day, Sunday, it rained heavily all day. Rain was a rare occurrence, but it was welcomed, especially by the local farmers. The steady downpour provided a soothing backdrop to the otherwise tense atmosphere that had settled over our home. Despite the rain, we decided to drive to Gunnedah, just over two hours away, to see my parents. It would be a nice two-day break from worrying about the Yowies.

The kids were excited about the trip, their spirits lifted by the prospect of seeing their grandparents. Ted and I, on the other hand, hoped that a change of scenery might provide some much-needed relief and perspective. We were also looking forward to getting a night's sleep without worrying about something entering the house.

As we pulled into my parents' driveway, the familiar sight of their home brought a sense of comfort. My parents were waiting for us on the porch, smiling warmly despite the rain. The moment we walked in, though, their expressions shifted.

THEY OWN THE NIGHT

They could tell something was wrong.

After settling in and enjoying sandwiches for lunch, the kids ran off to play in another room. My mother took the opportunity to pull me aside. Her concern was evident in her eyes as she asked, "What's wrong, dear? You and Ted look exhausted."

I sighed, feeling the weight of the past few weeks pressing down on me. "Mum, it's been…difficult. We've been having trouble with…something near the house. Something we can't quite explain."

As I recounted the events of the past weeks—the sightings, the noises, the attack on our home—my mother listened intently, her face growing more alarmed with each detail. When I finished, she looked at me with a mix of fear and determination.

"You have to leave that place," she said firmly. "It's not safe for you or the kids. Move in with us until you find somewhere else. We have plenty of room, and you'll be safe here."

Her offer was generous, and I knew it came from a place of love and concern. But the thought of uprooting our lives once again felt, in some ways, even more overwhelming than what was going on at home. "I'll discuss it with Ted," I said, appreciating her support. "Thank you, Mum. It means a lot."

She hugged me tightly. "You don't have to go through this alone. We're here for you, always."

I felt a wave of helplessness and exhaustion wash over me. Despite the temporary refuge, the fear of the Yowies loomed large in my mind. The rain continued to pour outside, a constant reminder of the unpredictability of our situation.

Later that evening, after the kids had gone to bed, Ted and I sat down with my parents in the living room. The fire crackled warmly in the hearth, casting a comforting glow around the room.

"We need to talk about what's been happening," I began, looking at Ted. "Mum thinks we should move in here until we find another place."

Ted nodded, his expression serious. "It's a kind offer, and we appreciate it. But we need to figure out what's best for our family. We can't keep living in fear, and we can't let the Yowies control our lives."

My father spoke up, his voice steady. "You're always welcome here. Take your time to decide, but remember, your safety is the most important thing. Everything else is just stuff."

We spent the rest of the evening discussing our options, weighing the pros and cons of moving temporarily versus finding a permanent solution. The support from my parents was comforting, but the decision was daunting.

As we finally headed to bed, I felt a glimmer of hope. Despite the overwhelming fear and uncertainty, we had the support of our family.

The rain continued to fall outside, and I couldn't help but worry that our stubbornness was preventing us from putting safety first.

24

IT SNARLED

....

Two days later, we were driving back home. The rain had cleared, leaving the landscape fresh and glistening, but Ted and I were filled with dread about returning to the house. Maybe that was a good enough reason to just up and leave. A home should be a sanctuary, and ours certainly wasn't right now.

As we pulled into the driveway, Ted suddenly remembered that we had forgotten to get milk on the way home. "I'll run out and grab it. Why don't you take the kids inside and get them bathed and ready for dinner?" he suggested.

I nodded. "Okay, sounds good."

I took the kids inside, and we immediately began our routine. The house felt colder and more foreboding than it had before, but I tried to shake off the unease. Hopefully turning the heat up would help.

The kids chatted happily about their visit with their grandparents as I ran the bathwater for Rachel and the shower for

James.

Meanwhile, Ted drove to the store, picked up the milk, and headed back. As he turned into the driveway, the sun was setting, casting long shadows across the property. Instantly, he noticed a figure on our roof. It was a Yowie, crouching there, its eyes glinting in the dim light. At first, it didn't see him, but the noise of the engine drew its attention. The Yowie turned, snarled at him, and then jumped off the roof, disappearing into the bush.

Heart pounding, Ted raced into the house, his fear evident as he burst through the door. "Michelle!" he called out urgently.

I came out of the bathroom; my hands still damp from bathing Rachel. "What is it, Ted?" I asked, startled by the look on his face.

"We had a Yowie on the roof," he said, his voice shaking. "It was right there, just staring at me. When it saw the car, it jumped off and ran into the bush. It was the ugliest thing I have ever seen in my life."

My legs felt like they were going to buckle. "We've been home less than 20 minutes," I said, incredulous. "Already they're harassing us."

"I know," Ted replied, his eyes wide with worry. "We need to figure out what to do. This can't go on."

We quickly finished getting the kids ready for dinner, trying to act normal for their sake, but the tension was thick. Every creak and rustle outside made us jump, our nerves frayed to the breaking point.

As we sat down for dinner, the kids chattered away, blissfully unaware of the terror lurking outside. Ted and I exchanged glances, the unspoken fear between us growing. Our home was supposed to be our haven, and it had become a place of dread.

25

SAFETY ABOVE ALL

After dinner, we put the kids to bed, making sure to lock their windows and draw the curtains tightly. Ted and I stayed up late, discussing our options and trying to come up with a plan. The recent encounter had escalated our fears, and the sense of urgency was overwhelming.

"We can't keep living like this," Ted said, his voice filled with frustration and determination. "We need to protect our family, whatever it takes."

I nodded, feeling a mix of helplessness and resolve. "I agree," I said.

As we sat together in the dimly lit living room, the exhaustion and stress weighing heavily on us, I finally voiced what had been on my mind. "Ted, I think we should cut our losses and go stay with my parents while we find somewhere else to live. It's not worth the stress anymore. I'm an emotional wreck."

Ted looked at me, his eyes filled with concern and understanding. "Are you sure? It's a big decision."

I took a deep breath, feeling the weight of the situation. "I'm sure. This place was supposed to be our fresh start, but it has become a living nightmare. We need to prioritise our safety and the kids' well-being. We can't keep living in fear."

Ted nodded, taking my hand in his. "You're right. We need to do what is best for our family and forget the financial and logistical implications. We'll start packing tomorrow and let your parents know we're coming."

A sense of relief washed over me, mingled with the sadness of leaving our home. But I knew it was the right decision. As we prepared for bed, the looming dread was tempered by a newfound resolve. We would find a new place to call home, a true sanctuary where we could feel safe and at peace. The Yowies were driving us away, but they hadn't broken our spirit.

26

MONSTER

....

That night, Ted and I finally fell into an uneasy sleep, the weight of our decision to leave somewhat alleviating our stress. The house was silent except for the occasional creak of settling wood and the distant calls of nocturnal animals.

Suddenly, Rachel's piercing scream shattered the silence. Ted and I bolted upright in bed, hearts pounding with terror. We raced into her room, fear gripping us like a vice.

Rachel was on her bed, as far back from the window as possible, her eyes wide with fear. "Monster!" she cried, her voice trembling as she pointed at the window.

As soon as we entered her room, that awful smell hit us, the same foul stench we had encountered before. I rushed to her side and gathered her into my arms. "It's okay, sweetheart, we're here," I whispered, trying to calm her frantic sobs. Then, I looked at the window and my blood ran cold. It was wide open, the night air chilling the room.

"Rachel, why is the window open?" I asked, my voice shaking.

She looked at me, tears streaming down her face. "I woke up and my room was too warm, so I opened the window. I laid back down and then I heard a cooing sound, like Auntie Tash's baby makes. I opened my eyes and looked at the window, and I saw this huge hairy arm reaching in. It went away as soon as I screamed. It stinks so bad Mama."

Ted stormed to the window and slammed it shut with a force that shook the frame. "Take her to our bedroom," he said, his voice tight with fear and anger. "I'll get James."

I nodded, holding Rachel close. "It's okay, baby, you're safe now," I repeated, though my own fear was threatening to start another panic attack.

Ted hurried out of the room and down the hall to James's room. I heard the sound of hurried footsteps and the creak of another door. Moments later, Ted came into the bedroom, carrying a sleepy and confused James.

"We're all going to stay together tonight," Ted said, his voice firm but soothing as he set James down beside Rachel. "No more sleeping alone."

I nodded, still holding Rachel tightly. "Ted, what if...?"

"I know," he interrupted, his eyes meeting mine with a mix of fear and determination. "But we can't think about that right now. We need to stay together and stay safe."

Ted quickly locked and barricaded the bedroom door, the kids settled down in bed with us, Ted and I lay beside them, wrapping our arms around our children, trying to provide some semblance of security. The tension in the room was unmistakable, each creak and rustle outside magnified by our heightened senses.

"Mama, what happened?" James asked, his voice barely a whisper.

"Oh, Rachel got scared," I replied, brushing his hair back gently. "But we're all safe now, and that's what matters."

27

WE CAN'T WAIT ANY LONGER

The hours dragged on, each minute feeling like an eternity. Ted and I remained vigilant, listening intently for any signs of danger. The wind howled outside, and the trees cast eerie shadows on the walls, but the house remained quiet.

Just as dawn began to break, Ted whispered to me, "We need to leave today. We can't wait any longer."

I nodded, my resolve strengthening. "I agree. We will pack up the essentials and be out of here as soon as we can. Whatever we don't take we will come back for later. "

When the first light of day finally streamed through the curtains, Ted and I quietly got up, careful not to disturb the kids. We began to pack, moving swiftly and silently, driven by the urgent need to get our family to safety.

As we prepared to leave, the reality of the situation hit me hard. Our home was no longer ours; it had become a place of fear and danger, belonging to the Yowies. The thought of leaving, of finally finding safety, eased my unsettled stomach.

By mid-morning, we had packed our essentials and loaded them into the car. The kids, though still shaken, seemed to sense the importance of what we were doing and cooperated without question.

Before we left, Ted and I took one last look at the house. "It's going to be ok," he said, his voice resolute. "We'll find a new place, a safe place. And we'll make it a home again."

I nodded, tears welling up in my eyes. "I know we will," I whispered.

We drove away, the house growing smaller in the rear view mirror. The road ahead was uncertain, but for the first time in a long while, I felt a sense of relief. We were leaving the Yowies and terror behind and taking the first step toward reclaiming our lives.

I don't know what Yowies are, why they were harassing us, or what we did wrong. But I do know one thing for certain: my family and I will never go anywhere near the Pilliga again.

EPILOGUE 1

MOVING ON

After a month of staying with my parents, we finally settled into a peaceful new life in the suburbs of Kempsey, NSW. The transition was smoother than we could have hoped for. The kids seemed to have forgotten or at least moved on from the terrifying experiences, and they quickly made a bunch of new friends at their new school.

Soon after we left our old house, we contacted the landlord and briefly explained what had happened. Surprisingly, they did not seem shocked and agreed to let us out of the lease without paying fees for breaking the lease. It was a small relief amid the chaos we had endured.

However, if they knew about the Yowies on the property and that was why the last tenants moved out, it makes me terribly angry that they didn't warn us, especially since we are a family with young children.

Three weeks after we left, Ted, along with a family friend, went back to gather the rest of our belongings. When they arrived, they were met with a devastating sight: the front door was smashed, and nearly everything inside had been ransacked. The smell was atrocious—the same overpowering odour we had encountered before, but even stronger.

The fridge door was open, with rotten food squashed on the floor, adding to the stench. The beds were beyond salvageable, reeking of urine. They grabbed what they could and got the hell out of there, leaving behind what had once been our home.

We are now much wiser about the unknown dangers that lurk in the shadows.

Our new life in Kempsey is a fresh start, a refuge from the terror we once faced. We are grateful for the peace we have found and the lessons we've learned. Our family is stronger for it, and together, we look forward to a future free from fear.

EPILOGUE 2

WHY WE DIDN'T RECORD EVIDENCE

In the aftermath of leaving the homestead and moving in with my parents, the few family members we told about the Yowies asked why we didn't record any sounds or take photos. In hindsight, it seems like an obvious step. However, living through those terrifying moments was an entirely different experience.

When the strange occurrences began, our primary concern was the safety of our family. The overwhelming fear and anxiety we felt during those encounters left us with little presence of mind to document anything. Our instincts were purely about survival and protection, not documentation.

Each night, as the sun set and the bush around us grew darker, our fear grew with it. The thought of grabbing an iPhone and snapping a photo didn't cross our minds. Instead, we focused on keeping our children calm and maintaining a semblance of normalcy amidst the chaos. Our home, which was supposed to be our safe haven, had turned into a place of constant dread and uncertainty.

Additionally, the experiences were often sudden and fleeting. A loud noise, a shadowy figure darting through the trees, the sound of footsteps just outside our window—all of these events happened so quickly that there was no time to react, let alone grab a device to capture it.

Moreover, when it first started happening, part of us didn't want to believe it was real. Documenting it would have forced us to confront the terrifying reality we were living in. Denial can be a powerful coping mechanism, and we clung to the hope that if we didn't acknowledge it fully, it might just go away.

We did have security cameras, and while they captured shadows and silhouettes, people wouldn't have believed us if we made it public. Just look at how many people are ridiculed when they do. We had enough stress to deal with and didn't feel the need to prove it to people we didn't even know. Furthermore, the Yowies were very intelligent; they knew exactly where the cameras were facing. Besides, I don't think the town's residents would have appreciated the attention anyway.

During this crazy time, we were simply trying to survive and protect our family. The idea of capturing proof for others was secondary to the immediate need to stay safe. Looking back, it's easy to see why people might question our lack of evidence, but during such fear and confusion, our priorities were clear: to get through each night and hope for a safer tomorrow.

As we moved forward, our focus remained on rebuilding our lives and finding peace. The memories of those nights will always stay with us, serving as a reminder of the unknown dangers that can lurk in the shadows.

While we didn't capture physical proof, the impact on our lives was undeniable and profound.

AUTHOR BIO

Luka T. Jacobs is an author with a passion for cryptids, particularly Sasquatch and Dogman. Originally hailing from Sydney, Australia, Luka now calls the picturesque Illawarra region of New South Wales home, where she resides with her partner and their cheeky little dog, Finnigan.

With a deep love for animals and a keen sense of adventure, Luka's fascination with the mysteries of the natural world fuels her storytelling. Drawing from her background in Graphic Design and Art, she brings a unique visual flair to her writing.

As an avid traveler and explorer of the unknown, Luka continues to seek inspiration from the wild and untamed corners of the world, eager to share her imaginative worlds with readers everywhere.

Facebook: https://www.facebook.com/lukatjacobs

Amazon: https://amazon.com/author/lukatjacobs

Website: http://www.LukaTJacobs.com

Take a sneak peak at Luka T. Jacob's first novel **"Night Of The Dogman: A Fight For Survival"** only <u>available at Amazon.com</u> for Kindle, paperback and hard cover.

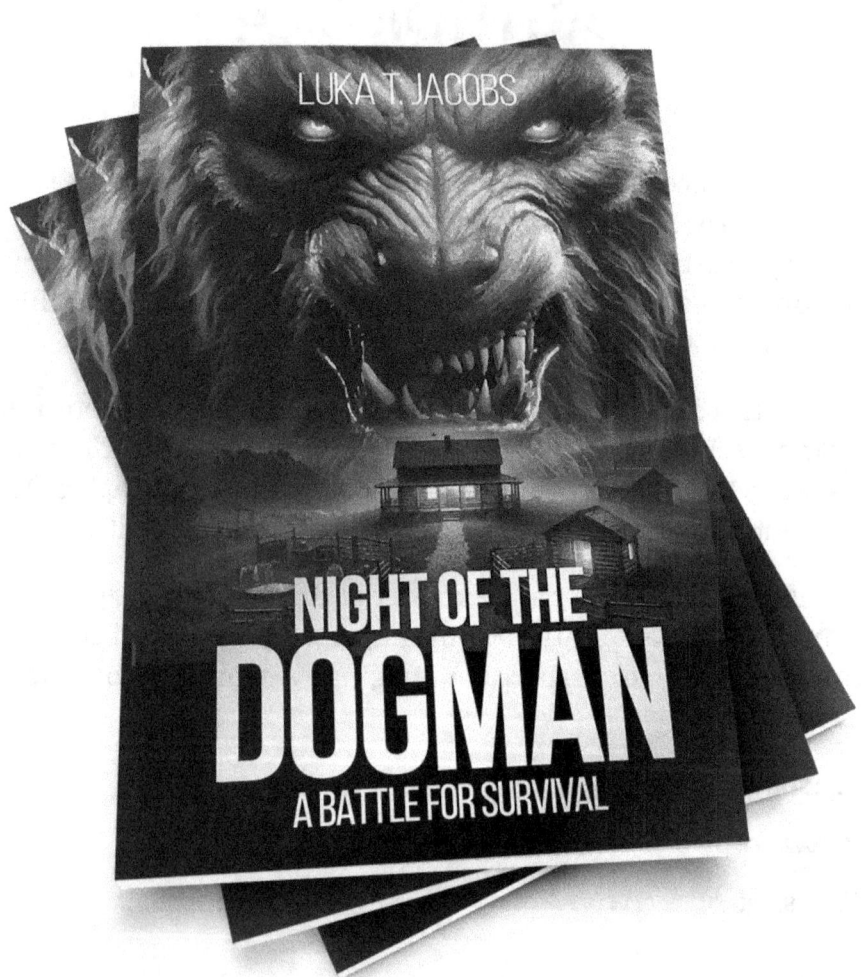

SNEAK PEAK –
NIGHT OF THE DOGMAN: THE SCENT

The night was draped in darkness, the moon obscured by thick, swirling clouds that seemed to dance with an otherworldly energy. The Dogman moved silently through the dense undergrowth, its senses keenly attuned to the faintest sound or scent that drifted on the air.

It had parted ways with its sibling under the cover of night, a silent understanding passing between them as they each embarked on their solitary hunts. For the Dogman, the urge to roam alone was primal, an insatiable hunger that gnawed at its very core.

As it prowled through the forest, the Dogman felt a surge of exhilaration coursing through its veins. There was a thrill in the hunt, a dark pleasure that pulsed with each beat of its heart. It relished the anticipation of the chase, the moment when prey and predator collided in a deadly dance.

But there was something more to the Dogman's hunger

than mere sustenance. It craved the fear and desperation of its victims, the sweet taste of terror that lingered in the air like a tantalizing perfume. It reveled in the power it held over its prey, the way their eyes widened with horror as they realized their fate was sealed.

As the night wore on, the Dogman's hunger only grew stronger, driving it further outside its home range in search of its next meal. It moved with a fluid grace, its movements silent and predatory as it stalked through the shadows.

But even as the first faint light of dawn began to creep over the horizon, the Dogman showed no signs of slowing. It was a creature of the night, and the night was its domain. With a hunger that could never be sated, it continued to roam, driven by an insatiable thirst for blood and terror.

As the sun began to rise, casting long, ominous shadows across the forest floor, the Dogman found itself on the outskirts of a town. It paused for a moment, its senses tingling with anticipation as it contemplated what the town might offer to satisfy its dark desires.

It knew that preying on the non-hairy ones within the town limits would draw unwanted attention upon itself. The last thing it needed was the scrutiny of the non-hairy ones with their metal sticks that roar and their endless pursuit of vengeance, recalling the sensation of being shot by one of those roaring sticks a few moons ago.

With a growl of frustration, the Dogman made a calculated decision to steer clear of the town for now. It would be more prudent to remain on the outskirts, where it could hunt without fear of discovery.

As it prowled along the fringes of civilization, the Dogman's keen eyes scanned the landscape for signs of life. It was searching for a challenge, something worthy of its cunning and strength.

Suddenly, a scent caught its attention—a scent unlike any it had encountered before. It was the scent of fear, but mingled with something else, something more elusive and intriguing.

Curiosity piqued, the Dogman followed the scent, its senses ablaze with anticipation. It moved with a purpose now, driven by a primal urge to uncover the source of this mysterious scent.

As it ran across the lonely fields, the Dogman's excitement grew. It could sense that it was drawing closer to its quarry, that soon it would come face to face with the challenge it had been seeking.

With each step, the Dogman's anticipation mounted. It knew that whatever lay ahead would test its strength and intelligence to the limit. But it was ready. It was prepared to face whatever challenges its prey had in store.

SNEAK PEAK –
NIGHT OF THE DOGMAN: A STRANGE SIGHTING

A week went by without incident. Adam sat on his porch, the warmth of his coffee mug cradled in his hands as he watched the sunrise paint the sky in shades of pink and gold. Fletcher lay at his feet, contentedly gnawing on a stick, unaware of the events about to unfold.

The wildlife of the Southern Missouri countryside stirred around him—the rustle of leaves as deer passed through the trees, the distant call of a bobcat, the quick darting movement of a raccoon. It was a scene familiar to Adam, a part of the rhythm of his daily life.

As Adam sat on his porch, his mind wandered back to his past life, reminiscing about the last time he felt truly content. It was a vivid memory of a day spent at the water park with Amber and Layla, just a week before their untimely deaths. The joyous laughter and playful splashing of his wife and daughter had warmed his heart in a way nothing else could. He cherished those memories of his family, holding them close like precious treasures in the depths of his soul.

Adam was lost in thought, his gaze unfocused, when something caught his eye—a dark figure swiftly moving across the rolling hills in the distance. Initially dismissing it as a trick of the light or a mere figment of his imagination, Adam's unease grew as he continued to watch. A chill ran down his spine.

Instinctively, Adam reached for the binoculars he kept nearby, raising them to his eyes and zooming in on the mysterious creature. It resembled a large coyote or coydog, its sleek black fur glistening in the morning sunlight. But there was something unsettling about it, something that filled Adam with a sense of dread.

As the creature ran, Adam could see the muscles rippling beneath its fur, the dog-like muzzle and large ears that marked it as a predator of the wilderness. But it was what happened next that caused his heart to skip a beat.

The creature halted abruptly, its gaze locking with Adam's across the distance. Then, to Adam's horror, it effortlessly rose onto two legs, displaying an eerie sense of comfort in its posture. Time seemed suspended as Adam stared into the creature's dark, penetrating eyes, witnessing it sniffing the air, igniting a primal fear within him. Adam couldn't believe what his eyes were seeing.

"*What the heck is that?,*" he whispered to himself, the words barely audible over the pounding of his heart.

Its head resembled a mix of a wolf and a German shepherd. Its coat appeared pristine, thick, and dark, likely dark brown or black depending on the light. Even from afar, Adam noticed its fur gently swaying in the breeze, its muscular and powerful body adorned with broad shoulders and sturdy legs. Its eyes, hazel or yellow, held a predatory gleam. Its elongated, muscular arms culminated in razor-sharp claws, exuding a menacing aura. Despite the distance and lack of size comparison, Adam could discern the creature's immense size.

And then, as suddenly as it had appeared, the creature dropped back to all fours and continued on its way, disappearing into the trees beyond. Adam sat frozen on the porch, his mind reeling with disbelief at what he had just witnessed.

Fletcher stirred at his feet, sensing his master's unease, but Adam could only stare off into the distance, his thoughts consumed by the encounter. A feeling of foreboding enveloped him like a heavy shroud, darkening the once tranquil surroundings.

Adam rose from his seat and made his way inside, the image of the mysterious creature burned into his mind. As he closed the door behind him, questions lingered in his thoughts: *"Why did that animal make me feel so fearful, like I hadn't felt before? It looked like a werewolf, but those aren't real!"* Despite his rationalizations, a lingering unease settled in his gut. He knew that something had changed, that the tranquility of his solitary existence had been shattered by the presence of something dark and unknown lurking in the shadows of the Southern Missouri wilderness.

Dear Reader,

Thank you for selecting my book from the myriad of options available. Your choice to explore my work is deeply appreciated, and your support means the world to me.

If you've found the book enjoyable, I would be grateful for your help in sharing it with others and leaving a review.

As a self-published author, reviews and word-of-mouth recommendations are vital for reaching new readers and spreading the book's message to a broader audience.

www.ingramcontent.com/pod-product-compliance
Lightning Source LLC
Chambersburg PA
CBHW050225100526
44585CB00017BA/2006